M
R...ah

Heinemann
LIBRARY

500 891 311

Little Nippers

www.heinemann.co.uk/library
Visit our website to find out more information about **Heinemann Library** books.

To order:
☎ Phone 44 (0) 1865 888066
📄 Send a fax to 44 (0) 1865 314091
💻 Visit the Heinemann Bookshop at www.heinemann.co.uk/library to browse our
catalogue and order online.

First published in Great Britain by Heinemann
Library, Halley Court, Jordan Hill, Oxford
OX2 8EJ, part of Harcourt Education.
Heinemann is a registered trademark of Harcourt
Education Ltd.

Editorial: Sarah Eason and Georga Godwin
Design: Jo Hinton-Malivoire and Tokay,
  Bicester, UK (www.tokay.co.uk)
Picture Research: Rosie Garai
Production: Séverine Ribierre

Originated by Dot Gradations Ltd
Printed and bound in China by South China
Printing Company

ISBN 0 431 18634 0 (hardback)
07 06 05 04 03
10 9 8 7 6 5 4 3 2 1

ISBN 0 431 18640 5 (paperback)
07 06 05 04 03
10 9 8 7 6 5 4 3 2 1

British Library Cataloguing in Publication Data
Hughes, Monica
Little Nippers Festivals My Rosh Hashanah
296.4'315
A full catalogue record for this book is available
from the British Library.

Acknowledgements
The Publishers would like to thank Chris Schwarz
and Corbis/Richard T. Nowitz **p. 23** for
permission to reproduce photographs.

Cover photograph of the children learning about
Abraham and Isaac, reproduced with permission
of Chris Schwarz.

The Publishers would like to thank the family
and school involved and Philip Emmett for their
assistance in the preparation of this book.

Every effort has been made to contact copyright
holders of any material reproduced in this book.
Any omissions will be rectified in subsequent
printings if notice is given to the Publishers.

Contents

Learning about Rosh Hashanah 4

In the kitchen 6

A special meal 8

Rosh Hashanah blessings 10

Apples and honey 12

Happy New Year 14

A new day, a new year 16

Blowing the shofar 18

Another meal 20

A walk by the sea 22

Index 24

3

Learning about Rosh Hashanah

I listen carefully to the story
of Abraham and Isaac.

In the kitchen

I help Mummy make two round challah loaves.

7

A special meal

Here come the challah loaves.

The table is set for our special meal.

Rosh Hashanah blessings

Mummy **lights** the candles very carefully.

Soon it will be my turn to take a sip of wine.

Apples and honey

I helped to slice the apples.

Mmm!

I hope the new year will be sweet.

A new day, a new year

I'm going to wear my white kippah and new clothes today.

The shofar is blown all over the world.

A walk by the sea

We enjoy being out in the
fresh air after our meal.

Look, the sea is taking the crumbs away.

23

Index

candles 10

cards 14

challah 6, 8

honey 7, 12, 13

kippah 16

new clothes 16

shofar 5, 18, 19

synagogue 17

The end

Notes for adults

Most festivals and celebrations share common elements that will be familiar to the young child, such as new clothes, special food, sending and receiving cards and presents, giving to charity, being with family and friends and a busy and exciting build-up time. It is important that the child has an opportunity to compare and contrast their own experiences with those of the children in the book. This will be helped by asking the child open-ended questions, using phrases like: What do you remember about …? What did we do …? Where did we go …? Who did we see …? How did you feel …?

Rosh Hashanah is one of the most important Jewish festivals. Special services are held at the synagogue lead by the Rabbi and a shofar, rams horn, is blown one hundred times. It is a New Year celebration that takes place over two days in September or October. Traditionally, apples are dipped in honey and eaten, and crumbs are thrown into moving water as a way of casting away sins so each person starts the New Year with a clean slate.

Follow up activities could include making a Rosh Hashanah card for a Jewish friend, finding a children's version of the story of Abraham and Isaac, trying some apple dipped in honey for themselves and making a list of all the special things the children do in the book.

GROW YOUR OWN

A Beginner's Guide

Ian O'Reilly

Grow Your Own – The Essential Guide is also available in accessible formats for people with any degree of visual impairment. The large print edition and e-book (with accessibility features enabled) are available from Need2Know. Please let us know if there are any special features you require and we will do our best to accommodate your needs.

First published in Great Britain in 2012 by
Need2Know
Remus House
Coltsfoot Drive
Peterborough
PE2 9BF
Telephone 01733 898103
Fax 01733 313524
www.need2knowbooks.co.uk

Contents

Introduction 5

Chapter 1 Getting Started...7

Chapter 2 Planning Your Garden....................................11

Chapter 3 The Indoor Garden..25

Chapter 4 The Vegetable Garden.................................. 31

Chapter 5 The Allotment...43

Chapter 6 Taking Care of Your Garden........................ 51

Chapter 7 Pests, Diseases and Problems...................63

Chapter 8 A Gardner's Year Planner............................ 73

Chapter 9 Plant Lists..79

Glossary 89

Help List 91

Introduction

Many people dream of growing their own fruit and veg, but are often put off by the time and space needed for a productive vegetable garden, they may only have a small garden available to them, or might live in flats and apartments with no outdoor space available at all.

In actual fact, what most people do not realise is that you don't need a lot of space available to produce fantastic tasting fruit and veg for your home – you don't even need to have an outdoor garden at all, but can utilise window sills, indoor greenhouses, patios and conservatories, even balconies! This informative guide will explain some of the many ways that you can utilise any space that you may have, and equip you with the knowledge you need to grow well.

Beginning to produce your own food can be a daunting task – many of us are put off by the gardening programmes that are full of detailed techniques, science and specialist equipment. Or a trip to a local gardening store can give the impression that it is a costly business setting up and maintaining a productive food source. This is not so, people have been producing their own vegetables at home throughout history, and one thing you will come to discover is that vegetable growers are nothing if not inventive in finding efficient and simple solutions to produce first-class, nutritious food!

When we produce our own food we have total control over what we want to grow and eat, and not relying upon whether your local market has a particular vegetable can be very handy indeed! We can radically reduce our weekly bills on food shopping (especially if we have a freezer to be able to store our produce over the winter), and we can ensure that ourselves and our family have a fresh supply of the essential fruit and veg that keeps us healthy.

Reasons to grow your own fruit and vegetables:

- Growing your own vegetable garden can save you money, and reduce your reliance upon businesses that may or may not have the produce you need.

- Growing our own is healthier for us, as the foods we bring to the plate are fresher and packed full of nutrients, vitamins and minerals, and haven't been sitting around on shelves and in delivery trucks for sometimes a week at a time!

- Growing our own fruit and veg can also be a good form of exercise – even in limited spaces.

- Producing a healthy food garden is good for the environment, as it encourages the beneficial insects like ladybugs, bees, butterflies and hoverflies, which are good pollinators for fruiting plants and won't eat your crop at the same time.

- Having an active garden through the year, especially for families, is a wonderful way to get people interested in fruit and vegetables, and to teach the benefits of a healthy diet and lifestyle.

- The food you produce doesn't have to just be fruit and veg, but can also result in home-made jams, preserves, pickles, chutneys, wines and beers, syrups and cordials – even sweets!

- Last of all, but certainly not least, most people find that any form of gardening is recuperative and relaxing, and a balm to our often stressful and busy modern-day lifestyles.

Chapter One

Getting Started

Starting to grow your own fruit and veg can, at first, be a daunting task when we look at our bare soil or the wide lists of plants available to grow, but there are some easy steps to take to get you started and on your way to producing food.

You will find that some of the techniques you first employ, or the plants you start to grow, do not suit your particular needs or site – in fact every veg grower's garden is a work in progress, so do not get disheartened when you have to tinker with the format and the design – just think of the tasty fresh food you will be enjoying in a couple of months!

What do you want your garden to do?

The first thing to consider is what you want your space to be able to do, and what you want it to produce. It is a fact much lamented by even the most experienced of gardeners that they cannot produce every type of vegetable, fruit, salad or seed that they want to – and most try to specialise to cover what they use most often or what will become a special treat at harvest time!

Try to think of what you see your garden producing for your plate over the course of the year – we all have grand dreams but in actual fact the idea of producing one hundred percent of your food intake, particularly where space is limited, is unlikely at first. Think of which things you eat most often (potatoes, onions, beans and salads are most common), and see if you can cover some of that bill by producing it yourself in your space. Alternatively, you may prefer to specialise in only one type of produce – berries or fruits, and use them in a variety of ways to make fresh salad, jams, preserves, juices and even wines!

'Try to think of what you see your garden producing for your plate over the course of the year.'

The choice is entirely up to you, and you may find that just supplementing a little bit of everything (a plant or two), from roots and tubers to beans, fruiting vegetables and berries, a good way to start growing. You will come to find that some plants react well to your garden space and thrive, whilst others will dislike that environment and require different techniques – or that some plants you have an affinity for and can grow easily, whilst others are more troublesome. This is all a part of the process, and will help you to determine what is best to grow with your space.

Know your soil

The first thing that every successful food grower must do is get to know their soil. The earth that we are going to use to grow our food is different wherever we are in the world, and is actually made of lots of different compounds: minerals, elements, metals and organic matter. This collectively is known as 'soil'.

'The first thing that every successful food grower must do is get to know their soil.'

Depending upon its composition, your soil will either drain water easily or retain it – thus changing the amount you will need to water your plants. Your soil could also either be stony or fine, determining how much digging you want to do, and will also either be able to be classified as 'acidic' or 'alkaline'. Different types of plants prefer alkaline to acidic soils and vice versa – and if you know what type or earth you have, you can maximise your growing potential.

> Don't be deterred by the science! There are easy ready-made kits that you can buy from any good garden stockists which, in a couple of minutes tell you what type of soil – whether acidic or alkaline – you have.

Soil tests

Your soil testing kit will come with a test tube, a chemical reagent and a set of instructions. Choose a pinch of soil of about 3 inches or just under a finger's length under the surface. Remove any larger stubborn pieces of rock or material and crumble the pinch into the test tube. Add some water and the chemical reagent, after a few minutes the liquid will change colour which will indicate to you what type of soil that you have.

- Dark green – Alkaline soil, this will be good for spinach, beets, most green and leafy salads and broccoli – so consider using a patch of this soil type as a salad bed! Otherwise, if you want to grow other types of vegetables, and especially fruits, then consider adding soil conditioners, fertilisers and composts to change its ph level.

- Light green – Your soil is generally ph neutral and most vegetables will flourish well here. Consider adding more soil conditioners, fertilisers, compost and manure to enhance its productivity.

- Orange – Your soil is acidic and you will need to add quite a bit more soil enhancers to make it a productive place. Some plants are hardy enough to withstand acidic soil, and most will grow here, but for the best results consider adding soil enhancers, minerals, composts and manures in the form of raised beds.

Types of soil

- Stony soil – If an area of your garden is very stony (it is difficult to get even a hand fork into it), you may consider building raised beds on top, or turning that area into a rockery for herb and spice plants. Alternatively, you can dig out the area (removing the larger pieces of stone to use in a rockery, as drainage or as a border).

- Clay soil – Your soil will be deemed to have a high content of clay if it is of a grey to cream colour, and is obviously plasticine to the touch, just like clay. Clay is water-resistant and will hold water easily, which can be a good thing if you are prone to forget to water! Otherwise, consider adding some manure and compost to encourage free-draining.

- Chalky soil – Chalky soil is very pale and dry, and will have small chunks of crumbly white chalk. It is worthwhile adding quite a lot of manure, compost and soil conditioner to this type of earth to improve its growing capacity and to retain the right amounts of water.

- Peaty soil – Peaty soil is quite black in colour, crumbly to the fingers and can be damp or slightly wet. Peaty soil is actually very rich in nutrients and an excellent growing medium.

Summing Up

- Make a list of all the salads, fruits, vegetables, berries, seeds and beans that you eat on a weekly basis. See how many of these you'd like to try growing at home.

- Consider adding a few items which are solely 'treats' – strawberries, raspberries or current bushes are all easy to grow in confined or larger spaces and will be a delicious reward.

- Think about the herbs and flavourings that you add to any of your meals at home – fresh herbs of any variety are generally an easy and quick crop which can transform your meals, and can be used on an almost daily basis! Common herbs to grow are: garlic, mint, thyme, sage, coriander, dill, mustard and chives.

- Determine what type of earth you have got available to you, whether chalky, peaty, stony or clay.

- Take a soil test to see what plants would grow best in your space, (use chapter 5 in this guide to help you determine which plants would work best in your garden).

- Consider what you want to achieve with your garden, and how you could change your soil type to do that.

- If you do not have an outdoor space but are growing indoors then you will more than likely be buying compost from gardening centres – in which case you do not have to worry about your soil type as the pre-prepared compost will be rich with nutrients, free-draining and water retaining.

Chapter Two

Planning Your Garden

Now that you have deciphered your soil type, and thought about what you want to grow, it is time to start some serious planning of your future edible delights! You should consider a few things, namely:

- Available light.
- Space.
- Harvesting.
- Appearance.

Available light

The best place to grow vegetables (particularly soft fruits and berries) is in the south-facing area of your home. The very best option is to have a lawn or outside space which has a south-facing aspect. Otherwise, see which windows in your home direct to the south, and where any extra space (like patios, conservatories or balconies) are located. This southerly aspect will be your best growing area, it will make a salad crop into a quick-grow area and will also encourage soft fruits such as berries, apples and tomatoes to develop bigger and fuller bodies. All other vegetables and plants will benefit from the warmth and the light, but not as much as these suggested above. If you do not have any southerly aspects to your growing space, consider using a small greenhouse or polytunnel, and covered beds (with indoor growing you can enhance and mimic this intense light, so don't be worried!).

'The best place to grow vegetables (particularly soft fruits and berries) is in the south-facing area of your home.'

Space

Your biggest concern is going to be the amount of space that you have available to you. You might have a small outside area or a large one, or you may have large or small indoor areas such as hallways, spare bedrooms, sheds and front living rooms.

Your largest plants will obviously need the biggest space, and should be afforded plenty of light and plenty of air circulation around them – whether they are indoors or outside – to encourage the proper regulation of moisture and disease resistance.

Smaller plants can be placed together in lines, rows or rounds to allow sunlight to flow above and beyond them to the rest of your growing area. You should always consider in smaller spaces packing your smaller plants in to best utilise your space to start with, you can always prick weaker specimens out or thin the amount of plants later – something not so easy to do with the bigger plants.

'An important aspect to any garden is the vertical dimension.'

An important aspect to any garden is the vertical dimension – bear in mind that you can grow up walls, on shelves and from hanging baskets. Especially useful for smaller plants such as herbs, spices, strawberries and radishes is to grow these smaller plants on shelves or levels, behind which you can grow your larger plants. When considering this 'stacking' technique you may be amazed at just how much you can pack into a patch of sunlight!

Harvesting

When you are planning your garden you will need to consider what plants will be producing food when. This allows you to plan your space for access, and can ensure that you have some food being produced by your vegetable garden all year round!

Salads are very quick, leafy growers, and it is possible to grow from seed to first crop in just one month for some crops. For the best results crop every two months, or apply a 'cut and take' philosophy to salads; where you grow very fast-growing salad leaves and take as and when you need.

Appearance

Whilst the appearance of a vegetable garden is not necessarily the number one concern for many food producers, for a beginner it may be important; and it is uncommon to find any sort of gardener who doesn't take some pride in the look and appreciation of their veg plot! The appearance of your garden can reflect your personality and also the functionality of your garden; from large raised box beds for a practical vegetable gardener to small container pots for the unique and specialist grower.

Consider enhancing the appearance of your garden space by using interesting containers and pots (everything from terracotta pots, old plant pots, plastic tubs, bottles and old milk bottles even to old wash tubs, baths and old boots!) Also, ask yourself if you would like to enhance your experience of your garden by adding wind chimes (also scares away the birds which will eat young seedlings), or a small pond (which encourages frogs which will eat those pesky slugs).

It is worthwhile to be able to sit down somewhere in your garden space, somewhere in the shade and out of the way of any strong wind and rain. A few flowers here and there (purely for their ornamental values) will also vastly increase your enjoyment of your veg garden and have the added benefit of attracting the beneficial insects that can help pollinate your fruiting plants and who will also eat the unhelpful pests in your garden!

'Consider enhancing the appearance of your garden space by using interesting containers and pots.'

Choosing the right tools

There is a wide variety of tools out there available for use by the enthusiastic vegetable producer, and sometimes it can be confusing as to which ones you actually need, and how useful they will be in the long term! Currently there are many different types of tools which specialise in different areas, from pruning to digging. You will find that some tools are very good at certain tasks, and some good for more general use. As your area grows over time you will no doubt acquire many different types of tools for different activities and purposes in your growing area.

When choosing the right tools consider the following things:

- The weight of the tool. If a tool is too heavy for you, it can lead to aches and even injuries – and very heavy tools are more dangerous to work with if you do not have a good level of control over them. Whilst in the shop you should always be able to pick up the tool and feel the weight of it.

- The build of the tool. Is it made from plastic, metal or wood? Metal will probably be the most durable of all, as long as it has some sort of galvanising cover or coating on it to stop it rusting. These days all tools come with this kind of protective layer as standard. Look to see whether the tool is cheaply made or expensively produced – as a general rule with gardening tools; you always get what you pay for!

- Distinguishing features. Has the tool features, colours or enhancements which will make it stand out? This could even be a hook for hanging up, or a distinctive colour so that you do not lose it in the grounds, or confuse it with friends' or neighbours', tools are notorious for getting lent to friends often!

Digging tools

You will essentially need two different types of digging tools for working outside – a large fork and a hand fork. The larger fork will be used for turning and breaking up the soil, whereas the hand fork is more likely to be used for digging in plants and removing weeds.

You might also like to consider a Dutch hoe – which is a long stick with a blunt flat blade set at right angles to the shaft at one end. This is excellent at removing surface weeds from long rows and larger areas, especially come early summer!

Another useful little tool is a dibber – but is something which doesn't really need to be bought as it can be made or salvaged at home from old chair legs, larger bits of wood or curtain poles. A dibber is a rough cylindrical piece of wood which ideally tapers slightly at one end. This is used for making holes in the soil ready for planting or watering.

Pruning tools

There are three tools which generally comprise all that you need in the way of pruning equipment, and these are; secateurs, shears and loppers. The secateurs are small (palm-held) articulated snips with quite broad blades, and often a spring coil between the two different arms, used for pruning smaller woody pieces from plants – always get the types which have a lock mechanism (a simple push button) and a hoop for hanging, both of which allows you to store them in a safe manner. Any snips that need to be made for smaller material can usually be done using a sharp pair of household scissors.

Shears are larger chopping scissors (always use two hands) which are held horizontally onto the bush, hedge or grasses to cut larger swathes of plant material. They are also excellent for shredding plant material ready for composting. Shears are more dangerous however, and you should consider how you are going to store them safely, and whether you need them at all. Only really consider them if you have hedges and shrubs, a large composting project, or very wild grassy borders. The central nut which conjoins the two blades should always be adjustable.

Loppers are long-handled, articulated cutters (easily as long as your arms) which are used for particularly stubborn woody stems and branches. Again, loppers are not really essential for the vegetable grower and should only be considered if you have wilder land around your growing area which you will need to control or remove prior to setting up your space. Any stem larger than about two fingers' width should probably be sawn.

Clearing tools

Of most practical use for the gardener is the rake, which comes in a variety of sizes and styles – from large plastic fan rakes to thin T-shaped rakes. The metal rakes can be used to pull out detritus from your hardier beds with a gentle motion, and the larger fan rakes can be used to clear those autumn leaves (which make an excellent soil conditioner when composted correctly). The rake is only really necessary if you have trees surrounding your growing area, and have a large outdoor area with which to control.

An essential veg grower's tool selection

- Hand fork – Under £10.

- Larger fork – Approximately £20.

- Secateurs – £5-10.

- Durable work gloves – £5-10.

- Waterproof clothes or old clothes for work wear – Between £5 and £20.

- Water butt and watering can/old milk bottles – £10, or free when recycled!

- Compost bin – £10-15, or free when using recycled materials!

- Storage box, shed or container – Containers under £12, Sheds ranging from £80 approximately.

- First aid kit – Many kits can be bought for under £12.

Other useful tools:

- Dutch hoe – Under £15.

- Rake – Up to £12.

- Spade – Up to £20.

- Loppers and shears – Up to £12 per item.

- Dibber – Free, make it out of a thick stick.

- Small hand saw – For making raised beds, compost bins, frames etc., up to £15.

- Water hose/sprinkler – up to £12.

- Canes/bamboo stalks/long sticks – under a pound each.

Compost bins

Perhaps one of the most important things for any vegetable gardener is the composting bin(s). You will ideally need three sorts of containers, which should be open at the bottom and have an easy to open mechanism at the top. They should be made of something sturdy like wood or heavy-duty plastic, but can be made or brought made out of metal.

Compost bins should always be kept away from your house (in case of pests), and ideally should be in a sunny location. The reason why many vegetable gardeners choose three bins is that they commonly operate a rotation system where one bin is the 'freshest' and used daily, another is the older and its contents are left untouched to rot down, whilst a third is for woody elements or leaves for soil enhancers which take a considerably long time to mulch down.

Compost bins come in many different shapes in sizes – the most common available today being the large cylindrical bins with a 'cap' at the top and a 'vent' at the bottom with which to retrieve the finished product. Alternatively, you can make pallets into a serviceable compost bins, wooden boards, bits of tin, old tubs and large container boxes.

See the section in chapter 6 on composting for a further explanation of how to use compost bins, and what features you will need to produce first-grade soil enhancers!

'Compost bins should always be kept away from your house (in case of pests), and ideally should be in a sunny location.'

Water butts

The water butt is an often overlooked but very useful element for the vegetable garden as it stores collected rainwater to be used in watering the garden (but never for drinking). A large round plastic bin will suffice, but you can also use buckets and bottles if you are short on space. Ideally the water butt can have a cover with a smaller hole within it which can stop the majority of leaves, detritus and pests falling in. As water butts are so useful in the conservation of water they should always be considered!

Storage shed

Every gardener – whether vegetable or flower – should have a dry, safe place where they can store their tools. Even if you are an indoor gardener you can consider an old closet, porch or box for your tools. This will be where you can take off and store mucky clothes, sharp tools and potentially dangerous fertilisers. Even as an indoor gardener you will in time amass a variety of odds and ends, from bits of string, marking sticks for naming plants, old pots and containers, rags for wiping down tools etc. These should all be kept somewhere safe and not interfere with your home. Consider putting a bolt or a lock on any storage site.

First aid kit

Most houses have a first aid kit already, and your garden can ideally either have its own (kept where you store your tools) or should be accommodated for in this first aid kit. Whilst none of us wishes to think about the worst, it is always far better to be prepared, and things like plasters, bandages, creams and antiseptics are very important. If you have an outdoor garden you will doubtless experience knocks and grazes, nettle stings and perhaps itchy bites.

As a part of your first aid kit you should always consider some sort of antibacterial hand wash, soap or spray to be able to wash small cuts and grazes and to be able to wash your hands thoroughly after working with the earth.

Preparing the ground

Whilst many of us may wince at the thought of preparing large areas of ground, in actual fact for a long term, productive garden you may not need to. Remember that your vegetable garden is a work in progress, and over time you may come to add different beds, gravel paths and structures like outdoor sheds or polytunnels. For quick and effective outdoor gardening, in actual fact all you need to be able to do is to make sure that however many areas that you are devoting to vegetables are turfed and cleared of weeds before you can begin.

Following your plan, decide how many beds and where they are going to be placed – utilising the southerly-facing aspect as much as possible. You may like to mark out your beds with some string and sticks, placed firmly in the ground. Many gardeners at this point remove the top level of turf in that space if there was once lawn or grass in that area.

Another easy method is to place large sheets of heavy plastic or gardener's felt to cover your bed area and leave at least for a month or over a whole season (I know many gardeners who do this in the winter and remove the plastic come spring). This kills off all the weed seedlings in that area and keeps any plants down as it deprives them of the sunlight they need to germinate and grow.

Removing turf

- The best tool to use is a lawn-cutting spade (a long-handled spade with a sharp semicircular blade at one end).

- Force the blade through the top level of turf, weeds and grass and slowly rock the blade from side to side until you hear the tearing noise as it scissors through the grass roots. Continue in a straight line along your bed, until you have cut lines approximately 10 inches to a foot apart over your whole bed.

- Using a fork, fingers or a regular spade stab in under the grass roots and lift. With practice you will find that you can remove long 'ribbons' of turf which you can roll up and keep for composting, hedging, making borders or bug habitats.

- Only cut down between 3 and 5 inches with your tools – most of the grass roots you will discover lie on the surface of the soil and this should be plenty to remove the top layer of vegetation.

- Remove any large stones that are revealed and that will get in the way of your planting

- Consider composting or stacking the sods of turf to rot down for future use.

Select which beds need to be deep-dug

Some of our crops, like tubers and roots will need a fine, fairly stone-free soil in which to grow. This allows the plant to develop naturally and expand to its full potential. Crops like radishes, potatoes, carrots and onions all need this type of soil.

- For your root, bulb and tuber crops dig over your bed again in rows (you may find it helpful to use a board to dig alongside), remove any large and medium stones that you find.

- Keep the stones back in a place at the end of your garden. These can provide an invaluable rockery habitat for growing herbs and spreading plants, are very important for wildlife and can be used as pottage shards at the bottoms or pots or plant containers for good drainage.

Adding material to your beds

'Many gardeners add a mulch or a compost into the soil straight away, and then leave the beds for a whole season for it to be taken into the soil by the worms and tiny helpful organisms.'

Many gardeners add a mulch or a compost into the soil straight away, and then leave the beds for a whole season for it to be taken into the soil by the worms and tiny helpful organisms. Compost brought from gardening centres and compost made in your own home can be planted into straight away. A great advantage of this is that it lets you increase the volume of your bed without all the amount of digging! Consider using wooden boards to make raised beds and then spread the compost over your boxed, turfed soil to avoid extra digging!

- If you already have a lot of prepared compost at home (see the section in chapter 6 – it should a rich black and crumbly texture) consider spreading that over your prepared beds.

- If you are prepared to wait a whole season, mulch your beds straight away with cow, horse or goat manure (you can sprinkle chicken manure as well). This must be left for at least a month for it to break down and interact with the soil before planting).

- Remember that the more work you put in at this stage, and the more you enhance your soil, the better start you will have in your growing season, and a healthier environment with which to work on in the future.

Intensive methods to prepare your ground

As well as using black plastic sheeting to kill off the weeds, green manure and potatoes, there are several more intensive methods employed to prepare the ground prior to growing, these are more usually the use of a rotavator, weedkillers or a selective flame-thrower.

- Rotavators – Simple rotavators can be bought from many garden centres, whilst the more specialised ones will need to be bought from a gardening catalogue or a larger centre. The rotavator is commonly a petrol-driven or an electric push machine that you use to churn up the first four to five inches of the soil, and can be used to make furrows. Actually a descendant of the plough and the hoe, the hand-pushed non-mechanical rotavators will make furrows by turning over the topsoil on either side of their line.

  Whilst they can save you some work, you will also have to consider whether rotavators are useful for your growing project. You may decide to use one if you have a bad back for example (as with most you can remain in an upright, standing position). Rotavators do come at a price (between £100 to £600), and you will either need to have an electrical point nearby or be familiar with using oils and fuels. You should consider carefully whether you could do a better job with a fork, and whether you want to burn exhaust fumes in your garden (particularly if you are considering organic or permaculture techniques).

- Selective flame-throwers – Selective flame-throwers are ways by which we can kill the larger and more persistent weeds in our garden, and are commonly used by estates and stately homes to preserve the integrity of their gravel paths etc. The selective flame-thrower is quite a serious undertaking, as it will require careful handling, a knowledge of handling fuel and protective clothing, as such only the larger garden centres will generally stock them. One of the disadvantages to the selective flame-thrower is that, if you are not careful they can damage the soil and the plants surrounding your particular weed!

- Weedkillers – There is a large variety of weedkilling treatments available, such as sprays and supplements which you can dilute and add to your soil before you begin planting. Many of them have localised effects (for example are very noxious on particular plants), whilst some are general 'treatments' which will act in an antiviral way, killing off a genus of a particular fungus, spore or invader.

Whilst they are without a doubt effective, you must consider carefully whether you wish to use weedkillers at all in your gardens and allotments, as the toxins can effect your other plants, and can even be dangerous to your own health. Many weedkillers also have unseen side effects, such as sterilising the soil or killing the beneficial worms, insects, bird life or hedgehogs that can visit and help your garden.

Organic, green and permaculture gardening

There is a growing awareness in the gardening world about 'gardening green', or ways in which you can use your space to grow crops which are healthier for you, the environment and require less effort! These principles are encapsulated in the organic gardening principles and the permaculture movement.

Organic gardening

Many of us will have noticed that some of our food stuffs on the shelves have organic stickers and certifications attached. These refer to the fact that no harmful chemicals were used in the production of the crops (weedkillers, pesticides and insecticides or even chemical fertilisers). Noxious chemicals can be traced through the food chain and passed on into the vegetables that you are eating then to your own body – especially soft fruits and berries (which store the chemicals in their flesh). To avoid this unhealthy intake of heavy metals, we can choose to go organic, which means that we use chemical-free interventions in our garden. Instead of using weedkiller we remove the weeds by hand, and instead of insecticides and pest killers we can use natural alternatives or deterrence methods and by-hand removals. Last of all, we feed our crops with natural alternatives which only give the plants what they need to grow in the form of minerals and nutrients. One of the added benefits is that this style of gardening does not result in the harm of many beneficial insects and natural wildlife – many insecticides not only kill aphids and slugs, but also the blackbirds, robins and hedgehogs which feed off them, as well as the bees, butterflies and hoverflies we need to pollinate our garden.

- Consider using organic principles and organic products when setting up and running your vegetable garden.

- Use simple plant feeds made out of comfrey or nettles to feed your crops rather than non-organic plant food.

- Instead of insecticides consider using ladybug larvae, a little watered down lemon juice, fresh coffee grounds around plants to prevent slugs – see chapter 7 for further information.

Permaculture gardening

Permaculture gardening – originating on techniques developed in Australia but based on ancient principles, means working in a much closer way with the soil and the environment rather than battling it (as it can sometimes feel when being a gardener!). Some of the main principles are: use the landscape as appropriate for the right crops (or, do not try to grow foodstuffs which are completely unsuited to your land type), use companion planting and other helpful plants to attract beneficial insects and pest repellents, and scatter your planting so each plant can have a beneficial impact upon its neighbour rather than the 'monoculture' method of farming that we often have today.

- In your food beds use two or three different crops in the same bed – this avoids a disease or a pest decimating your whole crop! Also, by using companion planting your selection of plants can encourage the right uptake of nutrients, deter pests and encourage beneficial wildlife to that bed.

- Utilise your space so your taller plants provide shade and cover for your tender, ground-loving plants.

- Rotate your crops so each crop will encourage the beneficial development of that soil (some plants fix nitrogen into the soil, whereas bulbs and tubers open up the soil and make it easier to work with in the next year).

- Utilise 'zones' so your nearest and most easy to get to areas are the crops that you use often, and the further areas of your garden require less maintenance, watering and are a haven for wildlife.

Summing Up

- Consider whether you want to use green principles in your gardening project!

- Make a commitment to not use dangerous insecticides, weedkillers or pesticides on your garden.

- Consider making comfrey and/or nettle juice as a food source for your plants.

- Add wildlife attractors to your garden (a bird feeder will encourage the birds to visit and eat the slugs), a pond, some old rotting logs for the beneficial insects etc.).

- Consider layering and stacking your plants so the tallest are at the back, with the smallest (ground-hugging plants) at their feet. Also, consider small greenhouses (indoor and outdoor) for their ability to be grown on shelves.

- Decide whether you want your veg garden to be beautiful as well, consider incorporating a few flowers such as sunflowers and marigolds.

- Draw a simple plan of your vegetable garden – which beds will be where, and what spaces you will be leaving free for future development. Also, how much space greenhouses, polytunnels, compost bins and water collection tubs are going to take up.

- Plan out the beds you are going to use for your vegetable-growing areas, where they are going to be and what plants (initially) you want in them.

- Acquire the appropriate tools for your type of garden.

- Prepare the ground by using black plastic sheets, weeding, a mixture of these techniques.

- Make sure you have set up a water collection system and a composting system.

- Remove turf.

- Use heavy plastic, old carpets or gardener's felt to kill weeds and prepare the ground for planting.

Need2Know

Chapter Three

The Indoor Garden

There are many ways to grow your own vegetables, and one of the purposes of this guide is to show you that you can produce an abundant vegetable garden even with limited space and inside your own home. This chapter will focus on gardening inside the home, and the many ways in which you can utilise this mostly forgotten growing space.

Indoor gardening

As previously discussed, there are many areas in your own home which can be turned into productive growing areas. In front of the kitchen sink, a bathroom window sill, a porch and hanging baskets can all produce for you nutritious delicious vegetables, and provide quite a complement to your weekly meals. Whilst most of what we consider to be vegetable growing constitutes farming – in actual fact, any of the plants that we grow outdoors we can grow indoors, given the right space and care.

When growing indoors, whilst you are free of hostile conditions such as pests and high winds, but you will have to manage the water intake of all of your plants. To do this select an old teapot or purchase a small watering jug and only use it for watering your growing crops. The soil should always be slightly damp to the touch, and you should never let it get dry or watery.

'There are many areas in your own home which can be turned into productive growing areas.'

Container gardening

To begin your indoor gardening project, select the area in which you wish to grow. It should be bright, have as much direct southerly sunlight as possible, and ideally be near a window with which you can ventilate the area. Select a range of tubs, containers and pots to start. Almost any container can be turned into a growing medium, from a margarine tub to a large plastic milk bottle, an old bucket or even a broken cup. Always remember that you should never use an object which once held dangerous or unhealthy chemicals – any container which has held any sort of pharmaceutical, cleaning or household chemicals should not be used. Ideally all of your containers should have drainage holes in the bottom, and thus should also have trays to collect excess water placed underneath.

- Select and thoroughly clean your container pots, soak for twenty minutes in hot water before drying. If possible, in the material use a needle to prick a number of holes a couple of millimetres wide in the bottoms of your pots for water drainage. Always take care when using sharp objects.

- Select old tin foil baking trays or the plastic lids to margarine tubs to act as collection trays for the excess water, underneath the container pots.

- In your growing area consider putting down some stiff cardboard (which you can remove and replace every season), or some durable plastic sheeting (a few sheets of tin foil can do at a pinch and also enhance the light output onto your plants).

- Select the plant sizes for your pots, salads are always better for the shallower pots, and singular plants for tubs and pots. Whilst plants like radishes, onions and potatoes can be grown in containers – always put these in the larger plant pots (at least a foot wide and deep).

- To start with, crowd your young plants together in your growing space, thin out and remove the unhealthy plants when they start taking over!

Window boxes

Another excellent way to produce quality edible plants indoors are the long, fairly deep window boxes that can be bought from any garden centre, or made and recycled from many second-hand outlets. Some you can simply place in front of your window (with a few heavy stones in the bottom), whereas others have wall mountings from which to hang on your walls by your windows. Consider growing herbs and salads in these as they are a fast, nutritious crop which you will use often, especially if it is in the kitchen window!

- Consider buying window boxes for your house and placing them either inside, outside or wall-mounting them. There are several available which come with ready-made hook fittings and only require a couple of nails with which to attach to the walls of your home. Always take care fixing them to the walls, and only use the tools that you are confident and familiar with.

- Consider stacking several window boxes above each other near your window and layering them with salads, herbs and strawberry plants.

- You will have to regulate the water in window boxes to a fine degree, so keep checking on them often (every couple of days) as you perform your daily chores.

- When it comes time to harvest – cut and enjoy!

Indoor greenhouses

Another marvellous invention which has benefitted many growers is that of the indoor greenhouse, which can be bought from most gardening centres at quite a cheap price. The indoor greenhouse is about a five to seven foot wire stand which also usually comes with a plastic cover that zips closed and open, and can be placed in the hallway, the kitchen, or any other light and sunny space. The advantage to the indoor greenhouse is it has a plastic cover so it captures moisture and heat very well, creating a mini hothouse environment which is perfectly suited to the growing of soft fruits and tender plants. By utilising its shelves as well you can stack numerous plants on top of each other in container pots and also have room at the bottom for storing old pots, work gear or tools.

- Consider buying an indoor greenhouse for your home, or alternatively you can make one out of wooden batons and heavy clear plastic simply by making a box-like stand and tacking the plastic sheets to it (remember to always keep one sheet only affixed at the top so as to get inside!) You can even use old glass display cabinets or glass-fronted cabinets as your indoor greenhouse (always remember to take care when moving and installing any object with glass).

'The advantages to the indoor greenhouse is it has a plastic cover so it captures moisture and heat very well, creating a mini hothouse environment. . .'

Balconies and patios

Balconies and patios are very useful sites for any food grower, whether you have a large garden or not, and whether you live in a large house or not – even if you live in a block of flats! Ideally suited to container growing, the balcony and the patio is a space where you can grow specialised and individual plants such as raspberries, strawberries, fruits and beans. As they are commonly situated to the southerly aspect of the house to maximise the sunlight, it makes the balcony and patio an ideal place for some of your favourite fruits.

▓ Consider affixing window boxes to the ledge of your balcony and by the doors that lead into your house. In the main flooring of your balcony you can install tables and shelving units to maximise your growing space.

▓ Remember that your balcony and patio is also a major light source into your home – carefully layer your plants that will still allow light to get inside your house (and any plants that are inside!)

▓ Remember to clean and sweep the floor thoroughly before gardening, as it is easy for rain and errant bits of compost to make a mess!

Indoor gardening task: All year round salad greens!

▓ Choose your favourite space that is 1) easy to reach and 2) has plenty of light – for the best results use a window box besides the kitchen sink or your food preparation area. Make sure there is plenty of direct sunlight.

▓ Consider using one of the long window boxes, or a row of smaller container tubs with a tin foil collection tray underneath. At a pinch a cut piece of guttering pipe will also do very well!

▓ Fill the container with some rich potting compost – it doesn't need to be very deep, between two to five inches will suffice. Potting compost bought from any gardening centre will be more than adequate to grow what you need, and will remain good for about two seasons. After this time consider adding more material, or emptying the contents into your compost bin and starting again.

- Select your seed – all year round salads are often a brand available from garden centres, and contain lettuce and spinach seeds. Consider using lettuce, spinach, chives and kale, or mustard and rocket for that peppery salad taste!

- Spread pieces of tissue paper on to a lid or plate by your window sill, and sprinkle the seed quite thickly (no more than a millimetre in depth) onto the tissue. Place more tissue paper to cover and sprinkle with water until the tissue is soaked, but not standing in water.

- Leave to sprout!

- Within a few days (up to a week) you will notice that about 70% of your seeds have sprouted. Prick out the strongest in little clusters and sow delicately into your compost. Make sure the compost is moist but not wet, and leave to grow.

- For an easier method prick and rough up the surface of the compost in your container to the depth of a centimetre, and thickly sprinkle your dry seed direct into the soil. Sprinkle over your seed with more compost and moisten.

- Within a few weeks you should have a fresh crop of tender shoots in your salad box – prick out the smallest plants and eat straight away and continue this process over the next few weeks until you have a pot of strong shoots.

- When your tender leaves have grown up to five inches, use scissors or your fingers to pick out salad leaves to use in your meals, as a salad or as a garnish. You should find that if you only take a handful every time you should be able to continue harvesting every few days. When the plant is failing to produce enough leaves, leave to let grow for a week to ten days – when the plant is exhausted stop, compost the material and start again! By using this technique, and staggering your planting so you start a second salad box a month after the first, you should find that you can have fresh, crunchy salads throughout most of the year!

Summing Up

- If you are going to have an indoor garden, start by choosing the space in your home with the most natural light and preparing it by adding shelves, old carpet of sheeting on the floor etc.

- Consider utilising your kitchen as a growing space by starting some cut-and-come-again all year around salad.

- Consider buying an indoor greenhouse, and maximising other spaces around your home – any balconies, window ledges, patios or hallways.

- Remember to control the water going to your plants.

Chapter Four

The Vegetable Garden

For the outdoor gardener there are perhaps more options available for growing tasty fruit and veg. Even if you have only a small outside area available however, you can easily turn it into a productive garden. Listed below are some of the options, you may want to consider a mixture of or concentrate on only a few for your space.

The vegetable garden

The vegetable garden, or veg patch can be a surprisingly productive place, if managed well. Generally the veg patch will not be a large space as you may also want your garden for other activities; growing flowers, playing games, or simply relaxing. This being the case the vegetable garden patch can be a way to supplement your diet, particularly at various times of the year, or as a way to experiment growing unique and tasty plants!

It is quite possible to grow one or two lines of onions, potatoes, leeks and lettuces in a vegetable garden – and come harvest time will drastically reduce your food shopping bill!

- When preparing a vegetable patch, always consider your available space and whether you want to specialise in just three or four crops.

- Think about how you are going to store your fruit and vegetables when it comes time to harvest them – a small garden shed, outhouse or porch are the very best options but a cool and dry cupboard, drawers or box will also do very well!

Climbing plants

One of the benefits to the vegetable garden is that you often have an area which is separated from the wilder world and so your slug and pest problems can be fairly controllable! Another advantage you will benefit from is that your boundaries (your garden walls or fences) will provide a very useful growing structure without you having to do the hard work of constructing frames!

First you must prepare these areas, remove any weeds and trash that can accumulate there and remove some of the turf (but be careful as you don't want to underpin or damage the walls themselves – consider piling lots of extra compost material in these areas to build up a good growing bank rather than digging).

Plant tall and climbing plants such as peas, beans, sweetcorn, raspberry canes, green gages or current bushes; you will find that you can restrain them by affixing them to your boundary with a length of string. Consider planting many plants in a row along your boundary and running garden twine in front of them every foot of height to give them something to grow up and to stop them toppling over into the rest of your garden! If you are growing current bushes (red and blackcurrants) you will find that you will be able to prune and train your bushes to run alongside your boundary wall by carefully selecting which branches to keep (the strongest stems closest the wall) and which ones to remove (the weaker ones and those that are growing out into your garden). By training your growing plants you will also be saving yourself a lot of time when it comes to harvest time!

'One of the benefits to the vegetable garden is that you often have an area which is separated from the wilder world and so your slug and pest problems can be fairly controllable!'

Raised (box) beds

One of the favourite methods for the vegetable gardener is that of raised, or box, beds. The advantages of raised beds is that they provide a natural barrier to the slugs and pests, protect your plants from the majority of spreading weeds, encourage some degree of heat inside the bed and allow you to specialise only on the soil that you intend to grow in.

- To make a raised bed, you will need some wooden boards, old planking or other sort of wooden box.

- Once you have removed the turf from inside the area and taken out the majority of the larger stones, you can place your frame upon the area and layer into it extra material, compost and soil from other parts of your garden.

- Your frame can be joined easily by adding a wooden baton at the 'corners' or you can simply place the boards against each other for your box shape and wedge them into the ground with smaller bits of batons or short sticks. Make sure that the box is held into the soil by either wedges or stakes. Alternatively, you can bank a little bit of the soil on the outside of the box and firm in with a foot.

- Raised beds should be considered for all of your vegetables, and are very useful for: potatoes, onions, parsnips, salads, roots, carrots and lettuces.

- Dig a trench around the outside of your box bed (about 6 inches wide, 3-5 inches deep). The soil from this trench can become extra material for the bed and produce an extra barrier for slugs and other garden pests.

- When using wooden boards, make sure the boards are water-treated by using environmentally-friendly wood oils and resins – this will save you replacing the box in a couple of years!

- Keep the wedges and spikes only a few inches deep – you may want to move the box to another part of your garden in the future!

- Fill the bottom of your raised bed with a layer of manure, muck or potato peelings and cover with plenty of new soil (at least six inches) to make a 'hot bed'.

- You should always be able to reach the centre of your bed with one arm outstretched, to make it easier to weed and harvest.

- Be creative! Old wine crates and broken or recycled cabinets can all be turned into smaller box beds.

Shelter beds

A shelter bed is a vegetable bed which has some form of cover (usually plastic) over it to create a warmer environment and protect it from the elements. This is usually a box bed with either blue polyethylene pipe arched over to make a semicircular structure, or simply bamboo canes making a frame which can be trussed together. Affixed to this can be some clear plastic sheeting.

The advantage of the shelter bed is that you can grow inside ground-hugging fruits, salads and crops later and earlier into the year, and encourage the growth of crops.

Shelter beds should always be considered for: courgettes, marrows, outside strawberries, dwarf beans, peas and squashes.

'The advantage of the shelter bed is that you can grow inside ground-hugging fruits, salads and crops later and earlier into the year, and encourage the growth of crops.'

> - Note down the eventual suggested height of your plants you want to go into the shelter bed, and raise your frame structure accordingly.
>
> - Weight your clear plastic sheeting down with stones or wooden batons for wind protection.
>
> - Dig in your polyethylene pipes or frame structure quite well (6 inches or more) as this structure will be affected by the wind. Higher frames (like fruit cages) will need to be dug in further, or perhaps some form of support like stands and props.

Frames

Frames come in many shapes and sizes, from large fruit cages to smaller tripods for individual plants. Frames are essentially useful for all types of beans, peas, fruits and vines. Your frame provides support and some wind protection for straggly climbing plants, protecting them from the wind, providing the plant something to climb and encourage growth, and allows you to harvest easier. Frames are essential for runner beans.

- A simple frame for a stand of beans consists of several bean canes (bamboo canes) placed at a 45 degree angle to each other, forming a triangle on the soil. Along the apex of these triangles place more horizontal canes and truss the whole structure together with string, twine or cord.

- Your frame should always be dug in at least 4 to 6 inches because, although the structure will have some integral strength, it will probably also be subject to strong breezes!

- You can tie string in 6 inches or one foot intervals stepping up the frame, making a 'ladder' that your plants can climb up.

- Especially useful for individual plants, you can make a tripod frame; place at least three bamboo canes in a tripod and truss at the top with string. The bottoms of the canes should also be dug into the soil as per the bean frame. Use again the string 'ladders' around the tripod to encourage your plants to climb.

Frames are especially useful for: beans, peas, tomatoes, sweet peas, sweetcorn, current bushes, raspberries and chilli plants.

Tips for frames

- Place fine gauze or netting abound your frames to protect against birds when it comes to harvest time!

- Try to use long pieces of string rather than many little pieces of string – this will save time later!

Rockeries and herb gardens

The final addition to any garden is the rockery or the herb garden – a method gardeners employ to utilise any waste or scrubby patch of ground into a productive area. Even if you have very poor soil quality or an unfavourable house placing, you can still create a rockery or herb garden out of pieces of pottery, broken bricks and stone.

Your rockery is a place where you can grow herbs and spices which may usually spread and take over a raised bed, but in this environment you can confine. This has the added advantage to make it easier for the harvesting of your plants, and diminishes the impact that weeds can have and easily drown out a herb garden!

- To create a rockery or herb garden, simply dig up the soil in your chosen site, consider adding a bag or more of compost, and into this mixture start adding fairly large stones, bits of slate and broken pots, and any stones that you have removed from your garden.

- Remember to keep adding compost and leave spaces between the largest rocks for the soil to take hold. After a while the soil will begin to take hold and you will have firm 'pockets' within which to grow your plants.

- As herbs and spices are quite hardy and do not essentially need very rich manure, compost or muck, you will not have to add more physical material to this type of bed, only plant food in the forms of comfrey water and nettle-infused water.

- Your rockery is ideally suited for the growing of: strawberries, thyme, sage, lavender and mint(s).

- Prick out any nettles as they form and add them to a nettle plant food!

- Consider planting some flowers like marigolds and evening primrose into your rockery as this will encourage the beneficial insects which will also eat some of the pests in your garden.

- Water with plant food every spring and autumn.

- Try not to use any objects which are too sharp when constructing your rockery, as this will make it difficult to take care of your herb garden in the future.

Greenhouses

Greenhouses are another much-loved addition to any vegetable garden, and if you are lucky enough to inherit a space which already has a greenhouse in place, then use it avidly! Greenhouses themselves were popularised in the nineteenth and twentieth centuries, and there are still many around which will only need a little love and care to bring them back to life. Alternatively, you can buy pre-fabricated greenhouses and construct them on site at your desired location. You can obtain greenhouses which are little more than six foot by six foot, up to fifteen foot by fifteen and can come with wooden panel frames as well as all-glass sheets.

▓ When sitting your greenhouse, always clear the ground and consider taking out larger stones to make the structure firmer.

▓ Always construct your greenhouse with care – consider employing a handyman or asking a friend to help you!

▓ When growing in your greenhouse, you can extend your growing season by up to three months – consider sowing your plants in February, and keeping a winter salad crop!

▓ Consider using raised beds and layering shelves inside your greenhouse to maximise your space and fully take advantage of the vertical dimension.

▓ Greenhouses, with their high light and heat concentration in the summer months (but lack of their insulation unlike the plastic of the polytunnel) make them ideal candidates for: chillies, peppers, tomatoes, vines, currents and other hot climate, soft fruiting plants.

▓ Remember to wash your greenhouse with a wet sponge and water to enhance the light uptake to your plants.

▓ Consider keeping the door or windows open ajar during the hottest summer months.

▓ Always take care when constructing, placing and working inside the greenhouse!

'When growing in your greenhouse you can extend your growing season by up to three months – consider sowing your plants in February, and keeping a winter salad crop!'

Outdoor gardening task: Growing raspberry canes!

- Select the sunniest side of your veg patch, which is also near the boundary wall, fence, or side of the house. This area should ideally be south-facing, and not have any immediately tall trees or bushes in-between it and the sky. If your vegetable garden is situated in a very crowded street or collection of houses, then you can also settle for the most southerly-facing side of a wall, fence or boundary. This will have the strongest and hottest amount of sunlight during most of your growing season.

- At the base of your boundary wall or fence, lightly turn over the soil (break it up into clods of earth and remove larger weeds such as briars, nettles and thorns).

- Make sure there is plenty of space for air-circulation in your chosen space – don't try to squeeze in your future plants next to overbearing bushes or aggressively spreading plants.

- Heap a line of compost (either bought from a garden centre or made from your own compost bins) in front of your boundary wall. Your line should be about ten inches to a foot thick, and shouldn't be directly against the boundary – bring it into the garden by a few inches.

- Consider boxing your new bed in by using old boards, bits of wood or the pre-made garden dividers that you can buy. Or you can use quite large stones (five to six inches in height) as your outer boundary. This will serve to keep your good rich soil inside your new bed and not let it be leached away when it rains!

- Buy or transplant raspberry canes from your local garden centre – you should find that young canes are relatively cheap and that you will be able to buy them individually or in sets. Place each cane about a foot apart and dig into your new big holes a bit over a foot in depth. Place each cane into their respective holes and fill with compost, compact and firm their seating accordingly – with a firm hand but not too tight. Give your new plants and the whole bed a good sprinkling of water if it isn't raining already, and leave to settle.

- Another good tip is, once you have brought your plants home and are just about to plant each cane into its hole, remove the root ball from its accompanying pot and place in the hole. Soak the root ball immediately and half fill the hole with fresh water before you fill back in with earth. Leave for a good few minutes to allow the root ball to drink in all the available water, and for the water to congeal the root ball into the hole you've made in your new bed. This gives the raspberry a little reservoir of food as you fill it back in, and acts as a good cementing agent to firm the plant into its home.

- Water your raspberry canes every few days when you notice that the surface of the soil is drying out, but do not allow the bed to become too soaked, wet or runny. Having placed stones or boarding, your new bed will help to keep the moisture and the soil inside the bed after watering and heavy rain.

- As your raspberry canes grow longer and taller (they can easily clear six feet) consider using string or garden twine, attached to your wall or fence and running fairly tight in front of the canes to hold them in and direct them up. This will keep them from flopping over into the rest of your garden!

- After a few months you will notice that they are ready to start fruiting, and that your garden is 'hedged' by a tall green canopy of fruit canes! You will probably find that you can grow other, smaller plants underneath the canes and moving progressively into the centre of your garden. This is known as staggering or layering your garden – and utilises an otherwise unused space (the vertical growing area against a wall).

- When they are ready, pick, harvest and enjoy your delicious fresh raspberries!

- If you have quite a line of four or more plants consider making raspberry jam, preserve, ice cream, cordial, or even raspberry-berry wine!

- Your raspberry canes will fruit (depending on the variety) in summer or autumn, and will always fruit on one year's growth of stem. After they have fruited and you have harvested the berries cut down the fruiting stem at the base (with a clean slanting cut, forty-five degrees to the soil). New shoots will appear in the spring, and your plants will continue to produce new fruit for many years to come.

- When planting raspberries, consider planting a mixture of autumn and summer varieties, and consider leaving a couple of spaces for a second planting of a few canes the following year. Within eighteen months you should be able to enjoy a yearly harvest of raspberries in summer or autumn, with the staggered ages of your canes.

- If you enjoy raspberries, also consider planting in a similar way loganberries and tayberries!
- Try performing this task in early autumn, ready for a crop in the next summer.

Summing Up

- When starting a veg patch, consider how much space you want to give over to growing vegetables.

- Prepare the ground as described in chapter 2.

- Consider only growing four or five different types of crop to maximise your productivity.

- Consider whether using raised (box) beds, frames, or shelter beds would be beneficial for your space.

- Try your hand at growing raspberries, berries or fruits along the boundary walls of your garden!

Chapter Five

The Allotment

Acquiring an allotment

Getting an allotment can be quite a challenge for a novice – but there are some simple steps you can take to ensure you have access in this larger growing space.

Many countries operate a system of allotments, notably the UK and America, and the methods by which you can hire yourself an allotment vary from county to county, district to council. You must always check with your local civic authorities about the latest guidelines and methods for acquiring an allotment.

A simple way to find out about allotments is do an Internet search with the words 'Allotments' and your area – such as your county, state, neighbourhood or city. This will put you in touch with the local authorities or others in your area who are using local allotments – and a simple email enquiry will often provide you with invaluable advice on how to get an allotment for yourself! If you do not have, or have limited access to the Internet, visit your local library, council offices or town hall and ask to speak to someone who may know how to register for an allotment.

Allotments are fairly large parcels of land which are kept in good faith by your local authorities for the pursuit of growing food – in some countries they can be bought and hired, but usually they are provided by your county council as a method by which you can support yourself and your family. Unless you have bought and own your allotment outright, they are not intended for business or commercial use.

The history of allotments is very interesting and is well worth researching for the dedicated grower, and date back (in the UK) to the Enclosures Acts and the modification of what is known as Common Laws into the Federal or Judicial Laws. Essentially, allotments are an agreement between the country and the citizen that they should always have the ability to use the land to sustain themselves, and were brought back by many governments in response to the Great Wars of the last century and the food shortages that resulted.

Allotments (originally) were the parcels of land outlined by Saxon law that were held in keeping by a village for the crops of that village, with the Norman Conquest and the development of the British Monarchic system, a lot of this land was refolded into manorial estates held by land owners and lords. Subsequent to the reign of Elizabeth the first and the stirring of the Renaissance, the needs for allotments grew as the rural poor communities became ever more depleted. It wasn't until the nineteenth century that the official Allotment Acts were passed, ensuring that for every 1,000 heads of population, there would be at least four acreage of land provided back to the poor for the growing of non-commercial crops. These Acts have been changed and reinstated in the two hundred years since then, the biggest boom occurring after the First and Second World Wars when the Crown saw fit to broaden the terms of this ancient agreement.

Allotments are rented or hired from your local civic authorities for a minute cost every year, with a few additional costs depending upon your local authority's guidelines. These may include access to water or the construction of a structure on your allotment. Please see your guidelines for further details.

In the United Kingdom there are groups of allotment associations which collectively hire the parcel of land, and in return for paying your fees you may hire that land as long as you abide by the guidelines. You local Association of Allotment Growers is a good place to start to enquire more about these. Some associations may require you to sign a contract or an agreement, which will stipulate the fees and expected use of the allotment, and generally be a common sense guideline for civil behaviour.

'Allotments are rented or hired from your local civic authorities for a minute cost every year, with a few additional costs depending upon your local authority's guidelines.'

What to expect from your allotment

You should always be able to expect certain things from your allotment, things which are essential to your ability to grow.

- A consistent water supply.

- A lockable entrance to your allotment, whether a self-built gate on your individual patch or an outer gate which is locked every night and opened every morning by a council official or head of your Allotment Association.

- Consistent and safe access to your allotment (for example you should be able to access your allotment area without great difficulty or danger; this may impact on road access or the street/alleyways and footpath access). As allotments are centrally owned by a governing body there should always be a level of safety maintained in accordance with health and safety regulations in your region.

Landshare systems

Alongside the availability of allotments, there is also often the option of Landshare schemes and policies, whether run by charities, private enterprise or personal agreements.

A Landshare scheme is one in which a gardening space is made available for the growing of vegetables, usually with some provision made to the land owners (such as a share in the produce), it can commonly otherwise be called a Garden Buddy Scheme or Organic Volunteering.

Each scheme is entirely individual, and you have to investigate its pros and cons before you sign up – but are generally very good ways of growing on land without spending too much money, and of course, getting to know like-minded people!

The most famous national Landshare initiative was instigated by the TV chef Hugh Fearnley-Whittingstall, and attempts to connect growers and land owners across the British Isles, with no fees attached! Another good place to start is the UK national organisation Transition Towns, who are a charity supporting downscaling and sustainability in all of its forms. For more information see the help list.

Questions For allotments

 How far away is it?

You should always consider how far away it is, and how you will get to your allotment or Landshare scheme when you have acquired it. Will the distance mean you have to use a car or a bus?

 Are you going to be able to devote enough time to it?

Linked with the above, you should also ask yourself how many hours a day and days a week you will be able to devote to your project. The preferable is about forty-five minutes every day (varying according to season), but many people also only go to their land space on weekends. If you cannot manage every few days, consider at least once a week spending a long morning or afternoon at your allotment or landshare.

'One of the added benefits to using an allotment is your ability to produce a high food turnover as your space increases.'

Using and planning your allotment

One of the added benefits to using an allotment is your ability to produce a high food turnover as your space increases. You will now easily be able to harvest leeks, onions, potatoes and carrots (at least) in their tens or twenties and not have to limit yourself to depending on the success of individual plants. Consider using rows or raised (box) beds for a larger concentration of food produce, you should find that you will be able to fit in quite a few of these into your space.

One of the best advantages to using an allotment is that you now have the space to try out any of the techniques previously mentioned in this guide, and room to experiment! You should start planning your allotment as per chapters 1 and 2 in this guide, thinking about the type of soil that you have and how best to use your space. Now that you have this space, instantly start considering installing a compost and a water-capture system, and think about using some of the largest growing structures and where they will complement your growing space.

The polytunnel

Polytunnels are a very useful addition to any serious vegetable garden, as they provide a hot environment which can extend your growing season by as much as four months every year. This is invaluable time in which to start off your vegetables early, and produce second and third crops throughout your year. Their hothouse environment allows you to grow soft fruits and vegetables more suited to a Mediterranean climate, and to continue growing salads and crops even through the winter months, and makes the dream of the sustainable household much more possible.

The polytunnel itself is a large semicircular structure which comes in different sizes – from fairly small (ten foot long, fourteen, eighteen) to as big as twenty feet and longer. Likewise, the height of the polytunnel can vary from seven feet up to ten or twelve feet high. Understandably, polytunnels are considered to be quite serious undertakings, and should be constructed and sited with great care. The polytunnels themselves are most often bought in kits, and constructed on site – any good garden centre should be able to put you in touch with a source for reliable polytunnels. There are even today professional businesses who can supply and construct a polytunnel for you on your site, and many designed to your own specifications. Depending upon the exact length, the polytunnel is constructed by large frames over the doorways and 'ribs' along the inside in semicircular arches, some of the largest polytunnels even have internal support struts. A heavy clear plastic is stretched over the frame and is weighted at the bottom and is usually heaped with soil where the plastic meets the ground.

- When placing and constructing the polytunnel, consider employing professional handymen.

- Remove turf from the ground of the site prior to the polytunnel being put into place.

- Create a drainage trench (6 inches deep and wide) around the long sides of the polytunnel, and drainage routes can be drawn off away from the structure to prevent the ground becoming too boggy.

- Polytunnels are very useful for growing fruits, all year round salads, tomatoes, lettuces, vines, berries, squashes.

- Use raised beds inside the polytunnel for ease of use, and especially productive crops!

- Wash the plastic with a light brushing from a long-handled brush with a moist rag on one end. Remove any large collections of snow in winter, as this puts stress on the structure.

- When constructing the polytunnel, pull the plastic covering as tight as possible! This will give the frame some structural strength.

- Consider how you are going to control the water supply to your polytunnel, perhaps install a water butt which you can fill, or a funnel system to an outside water collection point.

- Plant early – even in mid-February!

- Remember that you are controlling the soil fertility and the moisture content of your structure – check often.

- Consider installing a door at one or both ends of your polytunnel, which you can leave open in the very hot summer and close in the winter.

Summing Up

■ Get to know your soil, and which part of your land gets the most sunshine for the longest daytime hours.

■ Start considering installing a compost system, a water collection system, and where you might store tools and equipment such as in a small garden shed.

■ Consider marking out a plot for the largest structures you can take advantage of; the greenhouse, fruit cages and frames, and of course the polytunnel.

■ When preparing your ground, think about sowing green manure in your freshly turned soil immediately.

■ Start by contacting your local county council and any of the associations mentioned in this chapter to work out the availability and suitability of an allotment for you.

■ Find out what the organisations rules-for-use and guidelines for using their allotment are.

■ Plan and prepare your ground as stated in chapters 1 and 2.

■ Consider installing a greenhouse, polytunnel or a shed to make more beneficial use of the larger space you have to play with.

Chapter Six

Taking Care of
Your Garden

As every food producer knows, a good crop is the result of good labour – and whilst you do have to pay attention and be involved in the development of your plants to avoid the nasty surprises of pests and diseases – you do not have to be toiling every hour of the day! Forty-five minutes, once or twice a day should be quite adequate for most gardens – and considerably less for smaller indoor gardens. There are some simple techniques with which you will become familiar with over the course of your growing year, and can be used either inside in the indoor garden or outside in a larger small-scale farming operation.

'As every food producer knows, a good crop is the result of good labour.'

Planting

Every plant will have its own specifications as to planting, and the backs of seed packets will always have a useful, simple guide on how to plant that particular type of plant for the best results. As a general rule of thumb all plants should be started out in a warmer environment to encourage speedy growth, and then hardened off by sitting outdoors for a few days in the early spring before final planting into your soil, bed or container. If you are using polytunnels, indoor gardening or other sheltered methods, you can consider planting out into your chosen site immediately.

Sprouting and tender plants

As per your guides on the back of your seed packet, your plant will have a period in its early life in which it is considered too tender to withstand the rigours of the outside world. At this stage (usually within the first month from sprouting or seed planting) the plant will need a greater amount of care and attention. Consider keeping these plants inside, in greenhouses, or under some sort of cover. After this stage, when the plant body is firmer and has more than its starter leaves you can consider potting the plant into its final destination – usually a much larger container or the bed outside where it will eventually fruit or flower.

Planting and potting-on

Each plant should be planted individually, so you can get a good look at the root ball and the young plant as you put it into the soil. Pay attention for damages, broken stems or fungus that has managed to get into the plant, and if this is the case consider composting the plant immediately or removing the unwanted material.

'When watering your plants, the best option available is a large watering can with a sprinkler attachment or a hose also with a sprinkler attachment.'

As your plant has been started in a container or plant medium you should leave and not water for one day to allow the soil to firm up and make the plant 'hungry' in preparation for its final position. Upend the pot or medium and firmly tap and massage the pot until the root ball and any loose soil slides out of the pot into your hand. Lightly clear the root ball of any excess (for tiny plants you won't need to do this – just make sure it has a good sod of its original compost) and place in a prepared pot or bed.

The prepared location should already have soil within it, and a hole or depression that matches the root ball of your plant. Water the root ball into the soil and fill in with spare compost, lightly firming the soil around the base of your plant. Give the plant an extra good watering to secure it into position.

Watering

When watering your plants, the best option available is a large watering can with a sprinkler attachment or a hose also with a sprinkler attachment. This allows you to drench the soil around the plant and not have concentrated jets of water which can damage supple plants and disturb the soil.

You should always consider how much water is needed per week (or day in summer) to keep the land moist but not wet, boggy or soupy. A lot of moisture comes to your garden in the form of rain and morning dew, and the watering that you will do is really a supplementary extra feed in the hotter months when the ground is prone to dry out easily.

> Watering is best done in the early morning (before the sun's heat) or the late afternoon/early evening. This will avoid such complications as scorching when the water is essentially boiled onto the leaves by scorching hot sun, and allows the cooler temperatures to suck in the moisture into the soil.

Weeding

Weeding is a task that can seem repetitive or annoying for the starting garden, but a good strong effort early on in your garden's history will pay dividends in the future.

By taking such precautions as raised beds and growing in containers and greenhouses etc., you will dramatically reduce the amount of weeding that you have to do in the future, and after you have initially cleared your ground and weeded it fully for a full growing season the only weeds that you should encounter in the future will be 'windblown' seed and opportunist weeds that will be easy to remove.

Growing in rows ensures that you can easily take out most of the pernicious weeds by using a Dutch hoe or a rake along the centre (unplanted) trench. Or a simple trowel will remove the weeds – which you can either compost immediately or leave to dry in the trench.

The best times to weed are just before planting out, and through mid-spring – by performing a 'blitz' on your bed you will be able to remove most of the weed growth, and will retard their return for another month.

It is important to catch weeds before they develop seeds and flowers, and before they strangle, drown or otherwise block your plants from the sunlight. By performing a thorough weeding once a month, or even every six weeks, you will greatly reduce their impact, ensuring you only need to do this four or five times through the year.

- Always wear gloves when weeding, as some plants – even small ones – can be prickly or be spiky to the touch.

- Use a trowel or hoe, not a spade or fork, when weeding, as you will be able to carefully and quickly remove weeds without damaging the plants you want to keep!

- Consider sowing ground cover plants if you have a particularly large area that needs weeding, such as radishes, strawberries and potatoes, which will have spreading or large low-lying leaves that will stop the sunlight germinating the weed seed.

'It is important to catch weeds before they develop seeds and flowers, and before they strangle, drown or otherwise block your plants from the sunlight.'

Mulching

Mulching refers to the practice of adding material on top of your bed, whether it is planted or not. It has many beneficial advantages, such as adding nutrients to your bed, improving soil quality, providing warmth in the cold months, retaining moisture in the hot months and detaining weeds as it covers them from the sunlight.

There are many different 'recipes' of mulching – and your choice will reflect your available materials and what you need to happen to your soil and your plants. Mulching can be performed to enrich a soil and to protect plants, as well as to defend plants from diseases and nutrient deficiencies.

Compost mulch

Simply adding some fresh compost on top of your bed (and around your plants, but not touching them) will add food and material to your bed. It should be performed early on to improve soil quality, and when needed to add food into the soil.

Muck (manure) mulch

Should be added on top of the soil and allowed to stand to rot into your prepared bed. Can be placed around (but not touching) your plants and should only be performed once or twice a year, as it can make your soil very rich in certain minerals. Excellent for fruiting crops.

Cow muck is very acidic and very rich, and should be left to rot for about a month before adding to the garden. Sheep, goat and llama muck is much less acidic, but should also be left standing for a week before addition to the soil. Horse manure is considered one of the best as it is hardly acidic at all, and can be added as soon as it is dry – a day in the sunshine should do it!

Rotted wood chippings

Should be added when you have a problem retaining moisture, but will certainly change your soil quality, consider only adding sparingly at the end of your growing season to enhance soil texture and prevent weed growth, and only apply a thin (one to two centimetre) layer.

> It is generally deemed best to mulch your bed sparingly during the growing season, and as a cure or a preventative during this time for various sickly or non-productive plants, and then mulch heavily your entire prepared bed in the winter to allow the fertilising properties to be rained and frosted into the soil before your next planting phase.

Composting

Composting is the essential tool for any professional or amateur gardener. It allows you to recycle unwanted material from your home and garden, and provides a rich source of food for your plants in the months to come.

Composting works be a combination of aerobic and anaerobic digestion, or with-oxygen microbes and without-oxygen microbes. The easiest and most common form of composting this guide will focus on is the with-oxygen digestion.

'Composting allows you to recycle unwanted material from your home and garden, and provides a rich source of food for your plants in the months to come.'

The various sorts of microbes (microorganisms) that digest your unwanted food will, effectively 'eat' what is there and turn it into pure constituent minerals and nutrients – or a rich, black, peaty substance which should be slightly powdery to the touch. They require air to live, and so the compost heap will require turning once in a while. It is possible to compost with anaerobic digestion too – with closed compost bins that do not require air circulation.

- Obtain a large compost bin or instead make a wooden box, open at the top and bottom (this can be nailed together out of old tin, wooden boards or pallets).

- Turn over the ground underneath the proposed site of the compost bin – not weeding or digging, just simply turning the earth over a few times to allow moisture to drain freely and the worms to come up into the compost bin.

- Start your composting off by using a mixture of green cuttings, food waste (soft food – absolutely no meat, fish or dairy), a little earth and some thicker material such as chopped up woody stems, very light twigs or the stems of dead plants. This mixture will provide the right amounts of nitrogen into your compost to ensure an active microbial flora.

- Continue adding the same sorts of material to your compost bin, if you have introduced a lot of one sort of material, remember that next you should introduce a different sort of material to keep the overall balance perfect.

- Keep your compost 'capped' by using a heavy old piece of carpet, a lid or wooden boards. This generates pressure and heat inside the pile.

- Turn your compost once every three months – this involves removing the lid and emptying out its contents, and then using a combination of a fork and a spade to put it back in again – this will add oxygen and air into the mix.

- Within six to ten months you should discover that the bottom of your compost pile has turned into a fine, black, slightly peaty substance, and shouldn't smell at all. This compost is rich and ready to be used!

Composting tips

- Use two compost bins for rotation purposes, once you have completely filled one 'cap it' and leave it – apart from the turning – for a period of two to three months. Do not add any new material to it. Any further compost is added to your second box which becomes your 'active' system. I have seen people use as many as three or four composting rotations in this way, and by the time they have filled the second or third, the first should be ready to be emptied and used!

- Periodically, in the hottest months add a little water to your compost.

- If you have enough privacy, and are not put off by this sort of thing – consider adding urine to your active compost heap during a discrete tea break whilst gardening!

Things you can compost:

Paper.

Light cardboard.

Grass cuttings.

Plant prunings.

Plant cuttings.

Most weeds.

Light amounts of sawdust.

Fine woody stems.

Thickened plant stems.

Soft fruits.

Any used vegetables.

Manure and muck.

Human urine.

Things you should never compost:

Bind weed.

Knot weed.

Himalayan balsam.

Plastics.

Detergents, chemicals, oils or solvents.

Cooked meat.

Fish and dairy products.

Animal scat (use a digester – details of which will be readily available from any good garden centre.)

Rotation

'Your crops in your growing space should be rotated every year if you are growing large quantities of the same plant in one area.'

Your crops in your growing space should be rotated every year if you are growing large quantities of the same plant in one area. Smaller plants, and larger woody bushes (plants like herbs and strawberries, other fruiting bushes, shrubs and trees) should not be rotated. The reason for this is that certain types of crops exhaust the supply of certain types of nutrients out of your soil, and will become susceptible to pests and, in particular, diseases. Luckily, different varieties of plants use and restore different nutrients, and so you can restore the balance by planting different things every year.

Roughly divide your crops into: brassicas, legumes and root vegetables. The rest of your crop which do not fit into these categories can be mixed into your general planting schema.

Brassicas:

Cabbage, cauliflower, calabrese, broccoli, kale, leafy beets, radish and rocket.

Legumes:

Beans, peas, french, runner's and broad beans.

Roots and tuber vegetables:

Potatoes, onions, carrots, swede, garlic and radishes.

Order of rotation

▨ Begin by planting legumes in one of your beds, as these will fix and release nitrogen into your soil. At the end of your harvest season, crop your legumes and then dig the hardy legume roots back into the bed with a thick mulch over winter.

▨ The next year in the same bed plant only brassicas, as brassicas and other leafy salads love the nitrogen-rich soils that produce thick leafy growth. At the end of the year, dig and compost the hardy roots and provide a thick mulch on that bed.

▨ That winter, or the following year, grow potatoes and root crops in the soil, as these will suck up the last remaining nitrogen and will open up the soil, providing air and circulation into your prepared bed.

▨ The following growing season (after you have cropped your root vegetables) return to legumes.

Rotation tips

■ As you will notice, it is possible to have three beds in constant rotation in any growing season, one with legumes, the next with brassicas, and the final with root vegetables. It is quite common for allotment growers and gardeners with larger gardens to operate a four-bed system, where the fourth bed is used, for the 'random' vegetable crops or kept fallow, or mulched and unused, as this will allow the soil to recuperate and digest the beneficial fertilisers more readily.

■ A good rule of thumb is to never grow the same crop in the same place for two years or longer.

■ Crop rotation is always a slightly hit and miss affair, but as you get more practised and more used to your growing area you will spot which places grow which crops better, and which crops seem to follow each other beneficially. Have fun and experiment!

Summing Up

- Start by utilising a composting system – work out where you are going to install it, whether you want a singular compost bin or a multiple-box bin system.

- Plan out your vegetable-growing year, when you will be planting certain plants and in what beds. This will help you devise your system of rotation.

- Organise a space inside the home, in a shed or under cover where you can sort out your pots, re-pot plants and do all of your preparation work before your plants go into their final locations in your vegetable beds.

Chapter Seven

Pests, Diseases and Problems

At some point in your gardening you will undoubtedly come up against some of the pests and problems that damage crops and hinder the growth of your plants. These could be anything from pernicious weeds, hungry slugs or even blight viruses. All of these things can have a massive impact on your growing capacity if left untreated, but if they are caught early can be nothing but a minor annoyance. In all instances, prevention is far better than cure!

Coping with pests and diseases

To maintain a healthy garden you need to pay attention to what is happening to your plants as they grow – if you are putting time into your growing space every day, this should be sufficient to spot problems as they start to develop, and take quick action.

Maintaining good soil fertility and applying a rotation system to your garden is also, for many gardeners, the only defence needed against most of the diseases and viruses that can affect a crop. Crop rotation and applying fresh material to your vegetable beds means that you are constantly providing a fresh supply of nutrients, every year, which healthy plants need to grow. A lack of fertilising soil and inadequate rotation leads to the build-up of the pests and diseases inside the soil. (See chapter 6 for more information on rotation.)

In most cases in the garden, when you have a serious problem it is a case of kill or cure – there is very little that can be done with wounded or diseased plants – sometimes you have to resort to burning them even, as adding the material to the compost will only spread the problem throughout your garden!

The good news is, however, that there are a range of tried and tested methods of prevention and every year thousands of acres of food crops are grown in the UK to successful result. Most problems in the garden – even pests such as slugs, aphids and rabbits will generally all have their favourite crop or plant which they will attack first – it is by identifying your weakest crop and protecting them that you can prevent most minor problems ever developing into serious ones!

Pests

Slugs

Slugs are the ubiquitous problem which face gardeners throughout the year. Unfortunately, it is impossible to fully eradicate them, as simply more will come into your spot! However, there are some tips on how to greatly reduce their impact.

- Pick off slugs every time you see them and dispose. If you do this every day you will be surprised how effective this can be!

- Slugs like moist and dank conditions – by introducing fine, dry and sharp elements into your space the slugs will find it much harder to move around and be deterred. You could use gravel paths in-between your growing beds, layers of dried and crushed eggshells, sharp sand, even coarse wool matting!

- Make it difficult for the slugs to get to your crops by using raised (box) beds. Surround each bed with a trench (10 inches wide by five or more deep). This trench can also be layered with some deterrents mentioned above and below.

- Slugs hate some chemicals – coarse rock salt, copper wire and coffee grounds. You can add these around your bed or individual plant but you must be careful not to add too much as salt in particular will damage your soil. Copper can be bought in strips of gardening copper tape which can be placed around plant pots, containers, or even entire beds.

- Grow enough density of crops so that it won't matter if the slugs chomp some!

- Slugs will go for the tenderest plants first – either grow sacrificial baby salad in an area around or away from your main crop, or only plant out your crops when they are a little bigger and hardier.

- Keep open and wide spaces between your vegetable beds (preferably gravel paths) as this will encourage natural predators like toads, frogs, hedgehogs and birds to eat your pests during the hours when you are not there!

- Use a combination of the methods mentioned for the very best results.

Aphids

Otherwise known as greenfly and black fly, aphids are tiny flying insects which eat the sap of beans, peas and all legumes in particular. You may notice them clustering on the underside of leaves or on the growing tips of the plants, which they will eat, weaken, and transmit fungal rots as the plant is damaged.

- Use a simple dilution of organic, or non-toxic washing-up liquid in warm water and gently sponge away the aphids. The washing-up liquid should be an earth-friendly variety and can be readily brought from any wholefood store. Otherwise a few drops of lemon or citrus oil, as well as tea tree or lavender in a solution of warm water will also work.

- Encourage their natural predators (ladybirds and hoverflies) by planting flowers (especially marigolds, sedum and buddleia), and leaving an area or an edge of your garden to grow wild with bits of rotting wood, piles of rock and wild flowers.

Caterpillars

There are a huge variety of caterpillars which can affect many of your crops, from the large to the small – and many turn, in later life, into beautiful butterflies (who in turn encourage cross-pollination of your flowers and trees). Some butterflies and moths are also considered to be rare and protected species, so if you find any that are particularly large (two or three inches long, a few centres thick), especially if they have spines or any coloured 'eyes' on their carapace, you should pick these larger specimens off and return them to a wilder part of the garden.

The most common, however, are the tiny threads of green caterpillars that are the larvae of the cabbage white butterfly, which will cheerily chomp their way through cabbages, lettuces, leafy greens and any member of the brassica family.

- Use the same weakened solution described for the treatment of aphids to clear the area of grubs and eggs.
- Encourage natural predators (birds, ladybirds and insects) by adding a wildlife area to your garden (with wild flowers, untidy bits of wood and stone), and around your brassicas. Plenty of space and light will encourage robins and other little birds to come and feed in your garden.

'Encourage natural predators (birds, ladybirds and insects) by adding a wildlife area to your garden (with wild flowers, untidy bits of wood and stone).'

Wireworms

Wireworms are tiny pests which live in the soil and burrow into root crops, causing damage to the root and proceeding rot. Wireworms live in the soil and are very hard to remove entirely, preventative methods should be taken instead.

- Ensure a vigorous crop rotation for root crops, to avoid the build-up of the pest in any particular patch of the soil.
- Remove ground-covering weeds and keep your plants slightly spaced out to prevent concentrations of damp conditions.
- Lift your root a few weeks earlier than generally suggested to avoid excess damage and build-up of the pest in the soil.

Cabbage root flies

The cabbage root fly is a tiny burrowing insect which lives on and around the soil of the brassica family, and lays its grubs at the base of the plants. The grubs burrow into the root ball and introduce rot into the plant. You will notice its effect on your brassicas by the sudden wilting and weakening of your plants.

- Grow the young plants inside collars – rings of plastic (or cut-up plastic water bottles) to prevent the flies getting to your plants.
- Grow brassicas under cover, in shelter beds, greenhouses, polytunnels or in containers.

Carrot root flies

Carrot root flies are low-flying insects which hop on to your carrots in the earlier parts of the year and lay their larvae into the surrounding soil. The larvae grubs burrow fine brown tunnels into your carrots which will warp, distort and eventually rot otherwise good carrots.

- Ensure a vigorous crop rotation every year to avoid the carrot flies finding your crops!
- Sow carrots in early summer to avoid the breeding season of the fly.
- Sown aliums (onions, leeks and garlic) because the smell repels the fly.
- Encourage a barrier or grow carrots under cover such as a polytunnel or a shelter bed to impede the flight of the fly.

Diseases

Downy and powdery mildew

Affecting brassicas primarily, mildew is essentially a fungal infection which spreads, like rot, when given the right conditions. The various forms of mildew will appear as fluffy spots either under or on top of the plant, alongside mottling and wilting of the plant.

- Ensure good soil quality and crop rotation by adding material every year to your beds – this will make sure your soil has free draining and discourages the mildew taking hold.

- Make sure that the brassicas are kept clear of weeds and spaced out to discourage wet and damp conditions.

- Water regularly and consistently, as sudden influxes of water or overwatering and underwatering and sudden dry conditions will encourage an environment suitable for mildew.

- Grow under cover, in shelter beds, greenhouses or in a polytunnel to make sure you can control the environment.

Mosaic virus

> 'Blight is perhaps one of the most feared thing which can affect a vegetable garden.'

The mosaic virus appears like a mottled mosaic of browns and yellows that disfigures the leaves of the plant, notably potatoes, beans, cucumbers and lettuces. The disfigured leaves wilt and eventually rot, and the bean pods turn black.

- Essentially, maintain a good crop rotation, as this will ensure that each plant has the right nutrients and prevents the build-up of the virus in the soil.

- Pick off and burn the infected parts of the plant and try to keep growing the main crop. In many cases beans and potatoes will still be healthy, even with a bit of mosaic virus. In worse cases, crop early when the virus first hits, and burn the worst parts of the affected plants.

- It is is essential that you burn and do not compost the mosaic virus, and that next year you plant your legumes or potatoes in a different spot – this ensures that the virus can be naturally neutralised in the soil and will not spread out to affect the rest of your garden.

Blight

Blight is perhaps one of the most feared things which can affect a vegetable garden – and many amateur gardeners dread its diagnosis in their beloved patch. In actual fact, blight is quite a common ailment, and can be negotiated and avoided quite easily with quick action. The blight virus is born on spores and affects tomatoes and potatoes – as the fungal virus is airborne the blight virus is resident across the UK, and if you are growing in an allotment (where a lot of the same plants have been grown year after year) you will have to take preventative measures early on in your growing career.

Blight appears as as brown spots on tomatoes and potatoes which leads to wilting and rot, and is especially virulent in the wet seasons.

- As always, ensure good crop rotation and only grow hardy and disease-resistant varieties of your plants. By choosing these strains this also creates a 'herd immunity' in your local area of growing plants, and encourages the fight against blight!

- Remove and burn all affected parts of the plant immediately, and provide a good fertiliser to the remaining plants (nettle or comfrey juice), to encourage healthy and resistant plants.

- Regulate the air flow by growing tomatoes and potatoes under cover – ensure that you do not have overly wet conditions.

- Alternatively, you can completely enclose your tomato and potato plants in greenhouses, growing indoors or in polytunnels and thus reducing their exposure to the spores from the outside air.

- Try to keep your plants alive and harvest early any uninfected plants. It is essential that you remove and burn all affected plants, to prevent the spread of the blight.

Companion planting

Another very useful method of preventative cure is that of companion planting, or using the beneficial properties of plants, herbs and flowers to attract and repel insects and diseases from your vegetables.

The principle of companion planting is simple; some plants attract the natural predators to the common pests, who do the work for you, other companion plants have a fragrance that deters pests, whilst some companion plants use different and complimentary nutrients in the soil of your vegetable patch.

To perform companion planting make sure that you have a space in front or beside your main crop with which you can grow your companion plants. You can either plant in rows (main crop, companion crop, for example) or you can push all of your plants together in a scattered fashion. Use the following guide to discern which plants accompany which crops.

Main crop – Brassicas

Companion crop – Sage, thyme, herbs, mint, chamomile, dill and rosemary. Late (winter) brassicas and early potatoes both do well together (but not earlier).

Helps by – Fragrant herbs such as rosemary, sage, mint and chamomile repel the cabbage white butterfly.

Main crop – Aliums (onions, leeks, chives and garlic).

Companion crop – Good with potatoes and carrots and lettuces.

Helps by – Masking the scent of carrots and lettuces against flies, but should never be planted with legumes.

Main crop – Legumes (peas and beans).

Companion crop – Cabbage and strawberries.

Helps by – Mutually beneficial uptake of nutrients.

Main crop – Potatoes.

Companion crop – Nasturtiums, raspberries and sunflowers.

Helps by – More resistant to blight, good air circulation and protection from the spores.

Coping with cold weather

Another problem that gardeners have to contest with is the cold weather – especially for late and early crops. This can come in the form of early or late frosts, or dangers for young and tender plants when they are first placed out into the garden. A common technique that gardeners employ is to use cloches – or hard plastic covers that come in a variety of sizes to place over your plants. They also have the added benefit of protecting against many pests too!

Cloches can be simply brought from any garden store – or you can even make your own out of clear plastic, old lemonade bottles (thoroughly cleaned). Consider attaching clear plastic to a small frame in the form of a shelter bed.

Consider using garden cloches for courgettes, marrows, berries, and any younger plants when cold weather strikes.

Netting against garden pests

A good technique to use to protect your taller plants and fruiting plants is to buy some garen netting and spread it over your plants like a blanket. There will be enough of a mesh gauze that light is let through, but it makes a difficult perch for birds, and the constant movement and air circulation is a deterrence to many of the flying insects and aphids. You should find that garden netting is quite inexpensive from any garden centre and many DIY stores, and you should be able to buy quite large quantities easily.

Use garden netting on any currants, soft fruits and larger leafing plants.

Summing Up

- Get to know the types of problems that can affect your garden by studying which pests might attack your particular crops.

- Check your crops every day or every few days for signs of damage, pests, diseases or problems.

- Consider using fresh compost (shop bought) if this is your first gardening experiments, and institute a vigorous rotation system for subsequent years.

- Act quickly on all signs of disease!

- Consider using companion planting and permaculture techniques in your garden.

Chapter Eight

A Gardener's Year Planner

Winter

The cold and dark months of the year is, technically, for the gardener, the start of their year for a well-planned garden. This is because the winter is the time that we can prepare the ground and add our extra mulches, mucks and fertilisers to create the most beneficial environment for our future garden. It is well worth considering starting your gardening project in the winter or autumn before your growing season!

December

■ Prepare your gardening beds by planning and plotting out any future beds, and digging over the ground. Spread a layer of muck, mulch or compost over your bed and lightly turn into the soil to help break down and enrich the prepared bed.

■ Sow early (winter) broad beans (only for mild winters).

■ Harvest late winter varieties of brassicas and potatoes.

January

■ Prepare beds by adding muck, mulch or compost over your prepared bed and lightly turning into the soil.

■ Sow onion sets indoors.

'The cold and dark months of the year is, technically, for the gardener, the start of their year for a well-planned garden.'

- Chit potatoes by encouraging the 'eyes' to start sprouting roots. Leave in a dry, indoor climate with plenty of light, this will give your potatoes a wonderful early start!

- Dig early bean and potato trenches about a foot to a foot and a half deep, and leave open to add the semi-rotted remains of your compost bin. Fill both in with soil in the spring.

February

'Spring is when we seriously start sowing our future crops, sprouting and starting tender plants, and creating our routine which will provide us with food throughout the year ahead!'

- Chit potatoes by encouraging the 'eyes' to start sprouting roots. Leave in a dry, indoor climate with plenty of light, this will give your potatoes a wonderful early start!

- Dig early bean and potato trenches about a foot to a foot and a half deep, and leave open to add the semi-rotted remains of your compost bin. Fill both in with soil in the spring.

- Harvest (hardy) winter brassicas.

- Start planning and preparing the ground for any future beds and structures such as bean frames, shelter beds, polytunnels and greenhouses.

- Sow early broad beans directly outdoors.

Spring

The spring is possibly one of the biggest and busiest times of the year for both the amateur and professional gardener. It is when we seriously start sowing our future crops, sprouting and starting tender plants, and creating our routine which will provide us with food throughout the year ahead!

March

- Provide an early mulch to your spring beds, a light covering of compost around your plants will ensure retention of moisture and an encouraging feed for your youngest plants.

- Start sowing your early plants – broad beans, potatoes, hardy lettuces, beetroot seeds and tomato seeds indoors.

- Start sprouting leek seeds indoors.

April

- Continue sowing potatoes outdoors.

- Sow beans and peas outdoors.

- Start sprouting all year round salads in containers (both indoors and outdoors).

- Utilise any indoor space to sow and sprout vegetables in container pots to ensure an early crop. Consider tomatoes, potatoes, peppers, peas and beans.

May

- Harvest early sprouted salad leaves, and sow again. Continue sowing tender salad leaves throughout the year.

- Protect against carrot and cabbage fly by planting out carrots in shelter beds or adding barriers (plastic boards) around these tender plants.

- Prick out weaker seedlings to strengthen your growing tender plants.

- Consider an early weeding of your vegetable beds.

- Continue to sow radish and beetroot.

- Plant out tomatoes, sweetcorn, peas, leeks and courgettes.

Summer

Summer is the time for the gardener when we can first really start enjoying our garden's fruits and foods. We have to perform some more extensive weeding, and can start experimenting with our plants by adding fruiting crops and training and pruning growing plants.

'Summer is the time for the gardener when we can first really start enjoying our garden's fruits and foods.'

June

* Plant out later crops of beans, tomatoes, peas, onions and salads.
* Start harvesting early onions, potatoes, salads and pea shoots.
* Plant in and pot on strawberries.
* Pinch out growing tips of established beans.
* Plant climbing beans.

July

* Harvest and sow salads continuously.
* Harvest early onions, potatoes and spinach.
* Fill in the gaps in your garden by packing in strawberries, herbs and salad plants.

August

* Start protecting and looking out for rots, mildews and blights on any of your plants.
* Feed tomatoes.
* Harvest beetroot, any early peas or beans or any other soft fruiting vegetables.

'Autumn is the time when the gardener can start extracting the most crops from their garden and preparing their garden for some hardy winter crops.'

Autumn

Autumn is the time when the gardener can start extracting the most crops from their garden and preparing their garden for some hardy winter crops. You should have a mind for what compost and muck you will be needing in the years and seasons ahead, as well as enjoying the fruits of your labour!

September

▦ Harvest sweetcorn, beetroot and celeries.

▦ Keep your greenhouse and polytunnels watered.

▦ Sow hardy winter salads.

▦ Harvest the last of your onions and any beans and fruits.

October

▦ Dig over your used vegetable patches, remove larger weeds and add soil enhancers.

▦ Sow broad beans and onion sets for next year.

▦ Sow hardy winter brassicas for the next year.

▦ Sow green manures in some of your vegetable beds to turn over and increase the amount of nitrogen in your soil. Consider doing this to the vegetable bed that is about to be a brassica bed next year, and the bed which is to be a legume bed next year.

November

▦ Sow winter salads in warmer conditions indoors, under glass or in a polytunnel.

▦ Plant winter onions, garlic, peas and broad beans for next year's early crop.

▦ Harvest brassicas and late leeks.

▦ Consider mucking or mulching your garden by spreading a thick layer of manures and mulches over disused vegetable beds.

Summing Up

▧ Consider starting your garden in autumn, late winter or early spring to get the most time to plan and prepare your growing area.

▧ Keep a continuous supply of salads all year round by sprouting and sowing lettuces, baby lettuce, spinach and peas.

▧ Prepare for your crop harvesting times and devote more time to your garden in the summer months!

▧ Consider filling the gaps in your garden whenever they appear with salads, radishes, strawberries and other quick-growing, edible plants.

▧ Plan out your growing year with a wall planner!

Chapter Nine

Plant Lists

Beans

Broad beans

Sow: February to May for summer and autumn crops, and November for an early spring crop.

Cultivation: Keep down weeds by using a rake or a hoe, and consider adding a seaweed solution before fruiting.

Harvest: June to September, when the bean pods are full.

- Tip: Do not manure, as this gives too many nitrates and prevents flowering.

French beans

Sow: April to June for autumn crops.

Cultivation: Plant four inches apart in little trenches, and crop when bean pods are young to ensure a second crop.

Harvest: August to September.

- Tip: Consider earthing up like potatoes to stimulate growth and protect young plants.

Runner beans

Sow: April to June.

Cultivation: Plant 6 inches apart and grow inside a frame. Pinch out growing tips when they reach six foot.

Harvest: August to September.

- Tip: Consider sowing extra runner beans or sprouting extra plants early in spring as replacements against slugs!

Beetroot

Sow: March to July.

Cultivation: Weed until plants are 2 inches high, and prick out clusters of plants until one strong beetroot is left from each cluster.

Harvest: June to October

- Tip: Plant near onions to avoid damaging flies.

Broccoli

Sow: April to July.

Cultivation: Thin out to 18-20 inches apart to ensure strong plants.

Harvest: February to May for early over winter crops and August to October for summer sown plants.

- Tip: May need staking if plants shoot up too fast.

Cabbage

Sow: February to June.

Cultivation: Sow thickly, two inches apart and use repetitive sowing for protection against slugs and to ensure all year round crops.

Harvest: April to October for summer varieties and winter crops.

- Tip: Give a liquid feed (seaweed, nettle or comfrey) when the ball-like heads are starting to form.

Carrots

Sow: March to June.

Cultivation: Sow thickly, but thin to three to six inches apart. Earth up overexposed root tops as the smell of the carrot encourages carrot fly.

Harvest: July to November.

▪ Tip: Grow with lettuce and chives to hide the carrots from the carrot fly!

Cauliflower

Sow: February to July for winter and summer yields.

Cultivation: Thin to 20 inches apart in a scatter fashion throughout your bed.

Harvest: April to May for hardy winter crops, July to October for summer sown varieties.

▪ Tip: Mulch and feed often, and protect the 'heads' or curds by using light covering of mulch.

Courgette

Sow: April to May.

Cultivation: Sow thickly in clusters and thin out to leave one strong plant from each clump. Do not spray water onto leaves, and make sure plant can be as free-draining and ventilated as possible.

Harvest: August to October.

▪ Tip: Spread hay or small sticks under the marrow and courgette fruiting bodies to avoid their contact with too much damp, or crop early.

Currants

Sow: Plant young plants when dormant, preferably October-November and keep mulches and protect over the first winter.

Cultivation: Mulch often with lawn clippings, train the first year's growth (selecting the strongest branches and pruning the weakest). Do this every two years.

Harvest: Harvest when fruits have turned a deep red, black, or white.

■ Tip: Plant against a frame or a stake to help pruning and training the fruiting stems.

Dill

Sow: April to May.

Cultivation: Thin to 12 inches apart to ensure strong plants, keep free from weeds regularly.

Harvest: Gather leaves when the plant is at least three weeks old, and for seed wait until seed heads have turned brown.

■ Tip: Helpful planting near cabbages.

Fennel

Sow: April to May.

Cultivation: Grow in soft soil, pinch out tallest shoots to encourage more leaves.

Harvest: Gather leaves as and when required.

■ Tip: Good to grow on its own, in containers as the fennel is antagonistic to most other plants. A very good digestive aid.

Garlic

Sow: March to April.

Cultivation: Plant the cloves pointed end up, 2 inches deep and 6 inches apart, earth up a little when needed.

Harvest: August.

Tip: Grow in the onion bed, and make sure the site is free-draining, as it is easy for early bulbs to become waterlogged.

Kale

Sow: April to May.

Cultivation: Sow thickly but thin to 45 centimetres apart and stake if necessary plants which have fallen over.

Harvest: January to April for over-winter varieties, November and December for summer sown crops.

- Tip: kale does not like rich feeding, and should be planted in a space previously used for beans and peas.

Leeks

Sow: Febuary to May, plant out June to August.

Cultivation: Make a hole with your dibber about 6 inches down and place seedlings in and water the hole. The leek will then grow to the size of the hole. Draw up soil around stems to blanch and have longer plants.

Harvest: January to April for over-winter varieties and November-December for summer-sown cops.

- Tip: When planting out sprouted shoots, consider trimming the long roots. Instead of harvesting – leave a few plants to go to seed and enjoy the spectacle! Also – leeks grown from original seed will be much bigger than any sown the same year.

Lettuce

Sow: February to June for this year's crops, August to October for winter and all year round salad.

Cultivation: Sow thickly and then thin out to six inches apart for the full lettuce bulb.

Harvest: April to October.

■ Tip: Continually sow lettuce under cover, in shelter beds and indoors for all year round growth. Eat tender leaves when young.

Mint

Sow: Plant root pieces 2 inches deep in a patch you are prepared to become a wild mint patch!

Cultivation: Add rotted mulches as a top soil when required.

Harvest: Cut leaves as and when required.

■ Tip: Plant in a container sunk into the ground to keep roots in check, or, alternatively divide, clump and transplant every two years.

Onions

Sow: Sow sets (tiny seed bulbs) in April to May, or sow onion seed January to April.

Cultivation: Sow thickly and then thin out to 4 inches to six apart, either in rows or clumps. Prick out until strongest onions are left.

Harvest: August to October

■ Tip: Consider earthing up onions a little if the onion body is showing. Try sowing salad onions (shallots) thickly and crop early. Dry well in a cool indoor climate before eating.

Parsnips

Sow: February to May

Cultivation: Ensure the vegetable bed is well dug with stone-free soil for unforked parsnips.

Harvest: January to March for over-winter varieties, or November December for this year's crops.

Tip: Sow radishes around parsnips to keep free from weeds whilst parsnips are growing, crop the radishes early and eat as salad vegetables.

Peas

Sow: Continuously between February and July for ongoing crops, and October-November for winter crops.

Cultivation: Sow thickly and thin to three inches apart, grow peas in a frame (a tripod of a fence line) and train up the frame with string.

Harvest: July to September

■ Tip: Consider sowing smaller trays of peas fairly continuously under cover and indoors, and crop the tender shots for salads.

Peppers

Sow: February to May.

Cultivation: Sprout under cover or indoors, and harden off inside your greenhouse, patio or polytunnel before finally planting in them. Give plenty of seaweed and high potash feed when fruit begins to develop.

Harvest: August to October.

■ Tip: Grow in a greenhouse for the best varieties, mist well to keep aphids away, but do ensure the soil is not too wet in case of mildews and rots.

Potatoes

Sow: March to May.

Cultivation: Dig a foot to a foot and a half deep trench, free from stones and line with old compost, newspaper shredding, mulches and a little more soil. Plant chitted potatoes in and fill trench. When good green growth has appeared earth up around the leaves to encourage the plant to grow taller and produce more potatoes.

Harvest: July to October.

■ Tip: Grow potatoes indoors in large container buckets, adding compost every now and again to the healthy green growth. When container is filled, harvest by upending!

Radish

Sow: January to July.

Cultivation: Sow thickly in rows and thin out to between one and two inches apart. Because they grow so vigorously, consider growing them as a space filler and a green manure to fill up your other vegetable beds!

Harvest: March to November.

- Tip: Good crop to grow with peas, lettuce and parsnips.

Raspberries

Sow: Plant dormant plants in November, but can plant until May.

Cultivation: Feed often with manure and mulch (at least every year). Cut down the strongest stem (or stems) after fruiting and allow younger stems to grow through.

Harvest: Harvest when fruits are a deep rouge-pink colour.

- Tip: Try growing against a frame, stake or balcony to help with pruning.

Spinach

Sow: February to August.

Cultivation: Sow thickly and thin to three inches apart when grown outside.

Harvest: Winter varieties January to March, summer varieties March to November.

- Tip: Consider sowing spinach all year round, thickly in container pots and indoors and cropping the tender fresh leaves.

Strawberries

Sow: Spring, throughout summer to early August.

Cultivation: Grow in a rockery or a well-drained soil where the plant can spread. Leave to let grow, and feed the soil every winter.

Harvest: Pick out strawberries every summer and autumn individually, every day from when you first see them.

- Tip: Grow in container pots that can hang from door frames or windows to prevent the mice from eating them!

Sweetcorn

Sow: April to June.

Cultivation: Keep weed-free and pile earth around tender plants to ensure strong growth.

Harvest: Corn is ready when the silk tassels at the end of the cobs have turned brown.

- Tip: Sow in complement to peas – sow sweetcorn in the centre of your pea patch in rows or circles, and allow the peas to climb up them.

Tomatoes

Sow: February to April.

Cultivation: Sow seed thickly, sprout and prick out until you have your strongest plants. Plant out under cover inside a shelter bed, green house or polytunnel in middle spring and feed regularly with comfrey liquid. Keep well ventilated and moist.

Harvest: June to October.

- Tip: Keep a close eye for blight and rots, and take quick action when first spotted. Gently shake plants to encourage pollination if indoors when flowers appear.

Turnips

Sow: February to March.

Cultivation: Sow thickly in small trench rows (an inch deep), and thin out drastically through the course of the season. Thin to three inches for earlies, and then once they have been cropped thin to nine inches apart for main crop.

Harvest: June to October.

■ Tip: Good to grow alongside peas.

Glossary

Chitting
Used on potatoes, the process whereby we encourage them to sprout more growing tips. Keep for a week or longer in a dry, sunny location.

Cloches
Material used to protect plants from the frost.

Composting
To create rich, fertilising soil from allowing plants products and garden waste to degrade in a controlled manner.

Dibber
A rounded stake that we use to make holes in the vegetable beds prior to planting – useful for leeks.

Hardening off plants
The process by which we make our tender plants used to the colder and wilder conditions outdoors. Take your plant out during the day and allow to sit in the sun. After a week keep the plant outdoors overnight.

Muck
Animal detritus, commonly from cows, goats and horses, used in the garden to fertilise the soil and feed the plants.

Mulching
Adding muck and compost to a bed (on top of the bed) to increase its fertility.

Netting
Using thin gauze or garden netting around plants to stop birds and other pests from eating their soft fruits.

Permaculture
Environmentally-friendly principles that encourage the grower to work with their garden rather than force it to perform in ways which is not natural for it.

Potting-on

The process whereby we successively transplant plants from one pot to another, when they have reached a good size and outgrown the old pot. You may need to do this a couple of times before eventually planting your crops outside in your garden.

Pruning

To snip off (with secateurs) the unwanted shoots from plants; including old or damaged shoots, or to encourage more prolific growth the next year. Always prune just above (to one side of) a growing nodule.

Rotation

Changing the order, every year, of your 'families' of plants by placing them in different beds. This encourages the soil to regenerate and reduces the risk of pests and diseases.

Weeding

To get rid of unwanted invading plants into your vegetable patch.

Help List

Allot More Allotments

UK national body helping people petition and create allotment spaces in the UK.
www.allotmoreallotments.org.uk/
Email: allotmore@gmail.com

Landshare

UK National Landshare Scheme, connecting growers and land owners together across the UK, tips, hints and social advertising available.
Email:info@landshare.net
www.landshare.net/

UK National Society of Allotment Growers

The UK national body that can help with any legal and organisational matters relating to your allotments, such as your rights, what to expect from your council, to setting up an allotment and helping you petition for allotment space from your local council.
National Society of Allotment & Leisure Gardeners Ltd., O'Dell House, Hunters Road, Corby, Northants., NN17 5JE
Tel: 01536 266576, Fax: 01536 264509,
Email: natsoc@nsalg.org.uk
www.nsalg.org.uk/

UK Transition Towns Network

Can help with a range of organisational and campaigning endeavours, from promoting green initiatives, networking and helping you set up an allotment or a permaculture group.
43 Fore Street, Totnes, TQ9 5HN, UK
Telephone: 05601 531882
www.transitionnetwork.org/

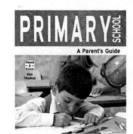
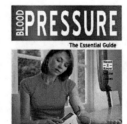
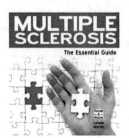